THE HISTORY OF MEDICINE
IN WISCONSIN

Copyright, 1958, by Walter J. Harris

All rights reserved — no part of this book may be reproduced in any form without permission in writing from the publisher, except by a reviewer who wishes to quote brief passages in connection with a review written for inclusion in magazine or newspaper.

Printed IN THE UNITED STATES OF AMERICA

The Story of
MEDICINE in WISCONSIN

By Walter Harris
Member of the State Historical Society of Wisconsin

"Life is short and art is long. The crisis is fleeting, experiment risky, decision difficult. Not only must the physician be ready to do his duty, but the patient, the attendants, and external circumstances must conduce to the cure."

Aphorisms

●

Walter J. Harris, Publisher
4317 Bliss Street, El Paso, Texas

GUYNES PRINTING COMPANY
EL PASO, TEXAS
1958

FOREWORD

This book, primarily a salute to Wisconsin's medical men, actually is an outgrowth of the 1936 Territorial Wisconsin Centennial inspirations absorbed at Madison by author Walter Harris while conducting a century of historical research for the benefit of Wisconsin Centennial posterity.

The book is a humble yet potent contribution to worthy Wisconsin enterprises. It is dedicated to history, education, culture, and *clean literature*. It aims to encourage the Wisconsin youth of today to become readers and writers in those fields in which creative art is somewhat currently lax, not providing enough desirable reading material.

The *Medical Story of Wisconsin* offers a huge bundle of charming regional history in capsule size—in both medicine and contemporary fields. It exemplifies "that mood which, with the lofty, sanctifies the *low*." It avoids burdening the story to the extent that the medical sequence is interrupted too often and unfairly.

In reading this book during high-school, college, or leisure moments, old and young will be inspired with a justifiable pride in the work thus far accomplished by the great medical men of our Badger State.

W. F. (Bill) Whitney
President and General Chairman, 1936
Territorial Wisconsin Centennial

Prologue

For research material and generous, unfailing help rendered him in the process of developing *The Story of Medicine in Wisconsin, 1634-1958*, the author is most grateful to:

The late Albert O. Barton, Madison
The State Medical Society of Wisconsin
Texas Medical Association
American Medical Association Journals
Volumes of R. G. Thwaites, State Historical Society
The late Dr. John Morris Dodd, Ashland
Dr. John T. Kendrigan, Northland College
Autobiography of a Surgeon by Dr. Dodd
U. S. Public Health Service
William Beaumont Army Hospital, El Paso, Texas
Milwaukee Sentinel, issues of 1836-1900
Evening Wisconsin Company's *Early Milwaukee*
The late Dr. Louise Phelps Kellogg, Madison
Travels of Henry R. Schoolcraft
Lewis Cass expedition report, 1820
The Chicago Tribune
U. S. Department of Indian Affairs
Ashland, Wis., Daily Press, issues of 1879-1925
Milwaukee Journal, 19th century editions
Encyclopaedia Britannica
Dr. Clifford L. Lord, State Historical Society
Associated Press and United Press
The Wisconsin Blue Book
Milwaukee Old Settlers' Club
C. H. Crownhart, State Medical Society
The late Dr. C. A. Harper, State Health Officer
State Health Officer Carl N. Neupert
The late Dr. William E. Ground, Superior
The Wisconsin State Journal
Hilma A. Harris, author's wife, whose typing and scholarly help were as inspiring as her past church-choir accomplishments.

ALBERT O. BARTON

In memory of the life work of Albert O. Barton, immortal historian, on whom The Lord smiled often, who deserves full credit for the publication of this book, having assigned the project of both research and writing to the author in 1944. At that time venerable Albert was in the process of publishing a book containing five chapters, one of which was medicine; but soon thereafter God summoned him for entrance into eternity, and his special book project fell short of reality.

Photo: Courtesy of State Historical Society of Wisconsin

The Oath of Hippocrates

"I will look upon him who shall have taught me this Art even as one of my parents. I will share my substance with him, and I will supply his necessities, if he be in need. I will regard his offspring even as my own brethren, and I will teach them this Art, if they would learn it, without fee or covenant. I will impart this Art by precept, by lecture and by every mode of teaching, not only to my own sons but to the sons of him who has taught me, and to disciples bound by covenant and oath, according to the Law of Medicine.

"The regimen I adopt shall be for the benefit and judgment, not for their hurt or for any wrong. I will give no deadly drug to any, though it be asked of me, nor will I counsel such, and especially I will not aid a woman to procure abortion. Whatsoever house I enter, there will I go for the benefit of the sick, refraining from all wrong-doing or corruption, and especially from any act of seduction, of male or female, of bond or free. Whatsoever things I see or hear concerning the life of men, in my attendance on the sick or even apart therefrom, which ought not to be noised abroad, I will keep silence thereon, counting such things to be as sacred secrets."

PART I

WILDERNESS WISCONSIN
When Medicine was Best Known for its Apathy and Neglect

The story of medical progress in Wisconsin—what inspiration!

What a cavalcade of historical fact! What discoveries! What blessings in this world of sin, suffering, fun, duty, and need!

In order to vision it all and to fully appreciate its vastness of influence and good, one must go back to our dim Wisconsin past—those centuries of pain, helplessness, and early death which preceded the start of true medical science.

Luckily, our lives were not of that era.

Death stalked every disease. From one wilderness generation to another, fate generally was cruel, causing stout hearts to suddenly stop beating as the result of agony that could not be abated.

Advanced surgery was unknown. So were effective drugs. Pharmacy was in need of a new learning. Its relationship to the sick was a subject of considerable apathy—as dull as scholasticism of medieval Europe.

Unknown was knowledge concerning ailments of heart, lung, kidney, gall bladder, appendix, intestines, and other parts of that material organism called the body. Any time an infection settled in one or more of these parts, it was an agency of destruction, allowed to poison the body as a whole.

This condition, relating to man's plight, was worldwide.

In 1634, when Jean Nicolet, youthful French adventurer, landed on a shore of Green Bay, wearing a Chinese robe and firing a pistol before awed savages in a bold venture which, he felt, was taking him to the Orient, there was inadequate knowledge in the world concerning the flow of blood.

Physiology, in fact, had been on its true course for only six years, or since the discoveries of William Harvey, English physician, who offered them to the world at large by way of a treatise which excelled the observations, hypotheses, and logical deductions of both Aristotle and Galen, the ancient Greeks. Harvey's theory concerning the circulation of the blood, readily accepted by the most eminent anatomists of Europe in 1628, was made public at a time when Captain John Smith was in a frightful struggle with mortality at Jamestown.

So, in that year when Nicolet became the first known white man to come into Wisconsin, medical science was in its first real stage of development abroad; and oddly enough, more than two and one half centuries were to pass in this country before medical progress as a whole could efficiently serve the sick.

A very slow transition it was. For 200 years—from the time of Nicolet's appearance at Red Banks to the establishment of Wisconsin as a territory—this transition was not actually under way.

Helpless men and women, with a burning stomach, choking respiratory disorders, a punishing backache or cough, quickly became invalids. Life for them was to end as soon as total exhaustion or poisoned blood stilled the heart. A man with a fractured leg was in a desperate struggle to survive pain. Death usually overtook him when a worn-out physique was subdued by gangrene. Undernourished Indians and white men alike were faced with the same health dilemmas.

Indians used spring flowers for medicinal purposes as well as for beauty and food. Certain plants were regarded as having healing powers. Other plants had the potency of magic, Indians believed.

Pussy willow roots, when made into a remedy, cured colic and other stomach aches. The roots were taken only from trees that had insect galls upon them.

Yet any remedy made from a root did not cure an Indian's appendix when it was ready to burst. It was not a potent enemy of streptococcus.

Intense pain, said the savages who practiced sorcery, was caused by evil spirits. To get rid of it, one had to fright-en unseen demons, chasing them away. During this process, harangues were shrieked in behalf of the thankful patient. They were regarded as necessary by sorcerers in their overall acts to make their versions of witchcraft seem effective, but rheumatism was still rheumatism in spite of these harangues. Ruptures were still ruptures. Gall stones were as troublesome as ever.

Old Indian traditions, rooted like the forest, kept proving that archaic learning was a dead process. Indians were meeting the terrors of disease in a manner that was obedient to ignorance, gullibility, and disservice; and the white men who had been seen in these remote wilderness areas as fur traders and explorers had not revealed any enlightening knowledge concerning cures for the sick.

Indeed the primitive practitioners had a regular course of treatment for every ailment, varying from hocus-pocus to prayer. Disabled indigents came to them with their gout, their smallpox, their painful throats and chests.

Synonymous with sorcery was soreness, which made the primitive backwoods life much harder to endure. Ignorance and superstition had to be combined with age-old fallacies in America to insure a livelihood for the medicine men of that day.

During the course of a long treatment, prayer was followed by song. Then came a so-called act of magic, with the medical faker spitting on his hands and placing the saliva against his patient's painful spot. In case of a sore, he put his mouth against it and sucked hard.

Failing to cure in this way, the sorcerer gave the patient an object which, he said, was the abode of an evil spirit. This object, called fetish, was in the form of a stone, a thorn, a weapon, or a feather. The patient grasped it for the purpose of crushing the spirit and quickly producing a cure.

If, by that time, the sick one felt revived and his comments reflected confidence in the medicine man's ability to cure, there was a mutual exchange of kind words. The sinning practitioner promptly asked for his pay.

And why not? After all, until better methods could be developed, the men of reddish-brown skin, straight-black hair, high cheekbones, and dark, brown eyes, who had established themselves as healers of the sick, had been utilizing their whims and knowledge in the generally accepted way, giving their best.

How did these savages restore lost hair for a bald-headed chief?

Like the hair-tonic specialists of this day, they just didn't. But some of them were known to place a thistle against a hairless scalp, and by way of a ritual, would imply that, perhaps, subject scalp had been purified and, as a result, hair would start growing again.

Medical history among these native Americans, however, was not all like this. In fact, great progress had been made by them in natural science. Many plants had been found to be good medicine as well as tasty food.

Roots from yellow-water lilies, for example, were used as poultices for cuts and bruises after being dried and powdered. The root of a white flower, known as blood root, was chewed by savages as a relief for indigestion. Furry leaves of the great mullen were smoked and dried, preparatory for use in soothing respiratory disorders. Inner bark from a slippery-elm tree was used to draw pus from a wound, and to further prove that an uncivilized race here was able in its own inherent way to develop many benefits in its study of natural science, a pike-fish tooth was used by our Indians in pricking the skin and then working into the blood-stream some medicine of their own make, which was intended to combat the internal agents of ill health.

A bitter calcium, made from a rare Wisconsin plant called jack-in-the-pulpit, was a relief for sore eyes; the best treatment for swollen eyelids was a medicine made from the roots of the large flowered trillium—a North Woods beauty in spring. This same flower became useful as a tonic for women. Finally it was a modern antiseptic for use in obstetrical care. Leaves from skunk cabbage, too, were fitted into our Indians' medical scheme as a whole, being used for poultices.

Yes, indeed, natural science was getting a dandy start in this part of the New World—a wonderland of water and forest, populated by only Indian tribes, a vast distance from the white colony at Jamestown, Virginia, where the first settlers from England already had made much progress as growers and manufacturers in spite of a heavy death toll caused by fever.

Everywhere man's struggle with fate was a subject of unlimited hazards and scope. In the field of health, as well as the soul, it virtually was a story of great length concerning pungency and disaster. In England it was the reason why 75% of all children had died under the age of five.

In 1661, when Radisson and Groseilliers, French fur traders, were building Wisconsin's first white habitation at the head of Chequamegon Bay, only men with giant-like physiques were able to survive the severity of that era. Fate had to be kind to them, preventing germs from entering their bloodstreams.

Germs, unknown in the world, would have ruined the Chequamegon fur business for those fearless adventurers if given an opportunity to enter the food or water which they consumed. Lifeless bodies would have marked the location of their crude dwelling place.

Some men were consistently lucky. Most of them were not.

As a missionary in a strange land, the 43-year-old Claude Allouez of France had been richly blessed in 1665 when setting up his log chapel on the shore of Chequamegon Bay. His heart and lungs and other vital organs had successfully withstood all the rigors of sickness, privation, and threat.

Not so fortunate was the kind, affable, Jesuit Jacques Marquette, who years later canoed on Green Bay and on the Fox-Wisconsin rivers with Louis Joliet, explorer-trader, enroute to the Mississippi to ascertain the source and the direction of that mighty waterway—the central trunk of a river system draining more than one-third the area of the United States.

Marquette, at 36, had managed to continue his work for God among the forest pagans in spite of hunger, dreadful experiences, snowstorms, sub-zero temperature, and fatigue; but a little later dysentery dealt him a fatal blow on a lonely beach near what is now Ludington, Michigan.

In that age, dysentery was a devastating ailment, having little or no mercy on the strongest of men, and those who suffered with it just had to fight it as best they could, with no medical men anywhere capable of treating it effectively. One complication followed another until death ended it all.

A century later, when ruthless fur traders from Canada were foisting deceit, rum, and fraud on sick, hungry, helpless, misguided, Wisconsin savages, a person in severe pain was no better off than the early explorers and missionaries whose life span suddenly had been cut short by sickness and the medical inefficiencies of mankind.

Nobody in the world yet knew what a germ was, and every time a disease-producing bacillus found its way into an appropriate work place through food, water, or air, spreading infection in a kidney, lung, or other vital organ, it was allowed to function without any disturbance.

Fur traders tried to disturb these germs with rum; but the mighty microscopic bacilli kept proving superiority over both rum and man.

Greatness and influence among men were of no value when a life was at stake. For example, as soon as a cold had disabled George Washington, the Father of our Country, causing him to suffer on his Mount Vernon bed, bacilli settled in his throat and then developed enough pain to make his illness critical. Within two days, on December 14, 1799, Washington's reserve energy had been used up. His family physician, in seeking to retard the pain, physicked him with molasses, vinegar, and butter. A blister of cantharides was placed against his throat. Leeches were used in bleeding him heavily four times. Suddenly an imperiled heart quit beating, and our first president's earthly service had come to an end.

For him, like all the rest of the people of his day, when a disease was of ill-fated torment, there were no effective drugs, no advanced knowledge concerning the treatment of disease, no urinalysis, no blood tests, no generally defined process of diagnosis, no physical examinations such as are known today.

Pain in one's appendix, intestines, or bladder was referred to as common, ordinary, stomach trouble, treated with impractical medicine, without any knowledge of surgery or even a need for it. A case of appendicitis merely was a rough battle with death, to end when an imperiled heart was made to stop by physical exhaustion and infectious blood.

In the fall of 1803, when Commi Michel Curot of Montreal, Canada, was portaging with his X Y Company crew along the Brule River, headed for the Upper St. Croix Valley in what was a part of Indiana Territory under Gov. William Henry Harrison, Curot referred to sugar as medicine.

Sugar, said Curot, revived a voyageur who suddenly had become ill. No doubt it was a case of undernourishment and fatigue, with some nutrition quickly furnishing enough energy to prevent a collapse.

Curot's food supplies, when entering the Wisconsin interior, consisted of corn, parched rice, and flour—not enough to ward off severe hunger before snowfall. There was no meat, no vegetables, no fruit, no milk, no eggs. The only cow in that region was on Madeline Island, owned by Michel Cadotte, a key trader, affiliated with the North West fur company.

So life for young Curot and his crew was to be a long, pitiful story of deficiency diseases, with the corn supply exhausted early in November and rice rationed on a basis of one pint for each voyageur each day, preparatory to the dreary series of hardships to be caused by snowdrifts and sub-zero weather.

Savages finally were starving. A dog owned by a fur trader ate two deerskins while striving to stay alive.

During that winter of fright, suffering, and well-organized sin at a trading post marked by the most wicked competition in fur-trade history, with the North West Company aiming to destroy the new X Y concern, Indian males asked for rum as a medicine every time they became ill. Indian mothers sought rum in behalf of sick children.

Medical treatment was not available for a young male savage after one of his ears had been severed by a hated rival in the cruelest of hand-to-hand encounters in sub-zero weather.

In a journal kept by Francois Malhiot, 28-year-old bourgeois of the North West Company, at his Lac du Flambeau post in the winter of 1804-05, there is mention of opium and rum for use in trying to relieve pain.

Once when gums and face had swollen as the result of an ulcerated tooth, weary Malhiot took 50 drops of opium, and when failing to get any relief, he drank a half pint of rum in what he termed one gulp.

In those days it was customary for a person suffering from a toothache to have someone pull the aching tooth with a pair of pliers; but Malhiot obviously wanted to avoid this type of ordeal.

Just how Malhiot, a victim of intense hunger, discouragement, cruelty, and fatigue, with pain in various parts of his body, managed to overcome the tragedies and fear of that Flambeau winter is a story of vast expanse concerning endurance.

In this matter of endurance, with emphasis on triumph over adversity, the overall Wisconsin story should prominently feature our James Duane Doty, who, as a young in-migrant from New York state in 1820, was given his first rigid physical test as a participant in that canoe expedition of approximately 4,000 miles, sponsored by John C. Calhoun, Secretary of War.

Doty and fate worked well together. Immortality had a place reserved for Doty, whose prerequisites for success in one of the most estimable expeditions in United States history were governed by faith. Doty's health was not impaired while undergoing the rigors of fatigue, undernourishment, treacherous-primitive travel, mosquitoes and flies, storm, heat, humidity, frost, and uncomfortable-sleeping conditions. All of this at a time when medicine was offering little or no defense against disease, being to mankind what the remote, isolated, Wisconsin wilderness was to a lonely explorer.

Smallpox, like a broken leg, soon meant a corpse.

For several months in that year of 1820, the health challenges were severe for Doty and his fellow expeditioners, who were under the command of 38-year-old Lewis Cass, governor of Michigan Territory, formerly a lawyer and a great war-time officer of the army, destined to become Andrew Jackson's Secretary of War, minister to France, United States senator, and Democratic nominee for President, with Zachary Taylor as his opponent.

What a leader! What self-reliance! What a producer of the pageant!

Health hazards? Why mention 'em to Cass? Or to other key expeditioners, including a West Point engineer and Henry R. Schoolcraft, topographer, geologist, and historian of New York, designated as official reporter for the Secretary of War. These men, along with an interpreter, a cook, soldiers, Indian hunters, guides, and voyageurs from Canada, long had adjusted themselves satisfactorily to perilous wilderness conditions.

Too, if sickness were to enfeeble anyone during this epic-like exploration, prompt medical service would be rendered. The doctor, named Woolcott, regularly assigned as an Indian agent in the shanty village of Chicago, was best known for his hemlock-bough juice, prepared by him without cost. His needs consisted chiefly of his favorite tree, an axe, a bonfire, and a kettle.

Incidentally, how would you like some warm hemlock fluid as a remedy for your gall stones, your inflamed appendix, hernia, diabetes, high-blood pressure, arthritis, or aching kidney?

Such ailments, of course, were unidentified in the days of Gov. Cass, and only physical giants could have done what the unique combination of adventurers under him accomplished daily from late May through late September and still live.

Shoving off at a community made up mostly of shacks, called Detroit, they reached what is now the harbor of Duluth by way of the Mackinac Straits, the Soo, the Portage Canal, and the Apostle Islands. The main route later in what was to become Minnesota was over the Mississippi, thence along the Wisconsin-Fox rivers and Green Bay, the straits again and back home.

The purpose of this trip was to obtain authentic information concerning Indian circumstances as a whole, to determine the identity of dominant Indian chiefs, ascertaining their locations, their habits, their plans, their feelings toward the United States and Great Britain. Other objectives were to negotiate Indian treaties, stop the warfare between the Chippewas and the Sioux, find the source of the Mississippi, purchase a site for a military post above the straits, study specimens of copper, make a map covering the topography for the entire region, ascertain the length, width, and depth of rivers, lakes, and bays, determine the extent of forest resources.

Throughout this vast territory called Michigan were approximately 8,000 white inhabitants, 1400 of which were in the capital at Detroit, the rest of them in isolated places far away, with little French settlements at Mackinac, Green Bay, Prairie du Chien, and Dubuque.

Along the water routes leading to these points of investigation went Cass and his canoe flotilla. Weakened regularly by intense heat and humidity, arduous paddling over choppy water, and portaging through jungle-like places on land, their improperly fed stomachs making known the seriousness of their plight, these official government cruisers were hit hard by sand flies and mosquitoes. At intervals they were forced to delay their water travel and go into the woods en masse to pick berries and hunt wild animals, turtle, and pigeon.

Both Doty and Cass developed lame knees and blistered feet, and whenever a party member became ill, he was given what the doctor said was a remedy—his decoction of hemlock boughs.

Without hemlock, the distinguished doctor was of little help.

Weeks later, when members of this expedition reached the source of the Mississippi, they found that a medicine made from the juice of the hemlock was being used extensively in an effort to save lives at a garrison occupied by the Fifth U. S. Regiment of Infantry.

Within a short time, scurvy had killed 40 of the original 100 men assigned there and had threatened to wipe out the whole regiment. It was a story of improper food and prolonged hunger, followed by months of only dried buffalo meat and Labrador tea as a ration. No other wilderness story concerning mortality that year could have been more appalling.

Prior to the call of death, helplessness of these men was best shown by swollen and bleeding gums, bluish skin, extreme mental depression, withered flesh and bones, ghastly stomach aches, fever, exhaustion, and despair.

During an early stage, juice from the hemlock lessened physical weakness and despondency. In time it tended to do harm. As a medicine, it became a pronounced hazard, causing nausea.

For these dying men, there was no hospitalization, no relief, no words of cheer, no effective nutrition, no sanitation, no hope, no self reliance, no advanced planning, no goals to seek.

In this remote outpost, critically sick soldiers were in a carnal environment which, of their own make, probably was the worst in army history.

A few hundred miles from them, southeastward, near the little French settlement of Prairie du Chien on the Mississippi River, some Indians were seen cooking skunk meat in order to avoid starvation.

Surely, in many respects, life here was comparable to that shown by Europeans when emerging from the late Stone Age. It was below the standards set by Sumerians 5,000 years before Christ. Yet it wasn't feared by Doty, the zestful explorer-recorder, who had decided to make this part of America his permanent home.

Born into a cultural environment during George Washington's first administration, Doty had faith in future Wisconsin. He had great faith in himself. For example, in 1824, when serving as the first Federal judge, with little to eat, plodding for many days over primitive, snow-covered, forest trails and sleeping on the ground, with only a blanket as a cover at night in frigid weather, he had no fear of distress or disease. Duty and self reliance kept leading him to success.

A painful rupture, a fractured leg, a weak heart, would have killed Doty quickly, regardless of where he was. In the only two white settlements to be found—Prairie du Chien and Green Bay—people seriously ill were as helpless as the ancient Greeks.

As usual, germs were undiscovered, and the man who was to make them known—Louis Pasteur, French chemist —was only a few years old.

The birth of Pasteur, in signifying the advent of world-important, medical discoveries, was not to bring forth any health benefits during Judge Doty's life. It also could not help Army Officer Jefferson Davis, who, as a young West Pointer, was assigned to Fort Winnebago at the confluence of the Fox-Wisconsin rivers, where he logged, cut lumber, and otherwise helped to establish the post.

Davis, too, was in that era when fate had to either keep disease germs away or permit them to send giants to their graves at an early age.

While assigned under "Rough and Ready" Zachary Taylor, embryo U. S. President, at Fort Crawford in Prairie du Chien, both he and Taylor became acquainted with the discoveries of William Beaumont, young army doctor and pioneer physiologist, whose salary was $40 a month and whose studies of digestion there formed the basis for nearly all modern medical research.

Beaumont's studies resulted from an accidental gunshot wound sustained by Alexis St. Martin, French-Canadian trapper, at Mackinac, Michigan.

St. Martin had in his abdomen a gaping hole which never healed. He was taken to Dr. Beaumont for treatment.

Noting that the wound had exposed a part of the injured man's stomach, Beaumont conceived the idea of studying stomach action; he tied a piece of meat to a surgical thread and then dropped it into the hole. A half hour later he withdrew the string. In this way he noted the process of digestion.

Beaumont studied the effects of alcohol and other substances on the open stomach. In time he made 200 or more experiments on gastric secretions, rates of digestion of various foods, the nature of hunger, et cetera.

In recognition of these great accomplishments in the wilderness of Wisconsin, the Texas Medical Association published the following in a recent issue of its "State Journal of Medicine":

Experiments and Observations on the
Gastric Juice and the Physiology of Digestion
WILLIAM BEAUMONT, M. D.,
Surgeon in the United States Army.
Plattsburg, F. P. Allen, 1833.

This work was the first exhaustive treatise on the physiology of digestion, which is described under the following heads: (1) Of Aliment, (2) Of Hunger and Thirst, (3) Of Satisfaction and Satiety, (4) Of Mastication, Insalivation and Deglutition, (5) Of Digestion by the Gastric Juice, (6) Of the Appearance of the Villous Coat, and the Motions of the Stomach, and (7) Of Chylification, and Uses of the Bile and Pancreatic Juice.

To appreciate the work, one must know something of the author and the circumstances. William Beaumont was born at Lebanon, Conn., November 21, 1785. Practically nothing is known of his boyhood. In 1807 he arrived in Champlain and began his study of medicine, teaching school and tending store to support himself. In 1808 he apprenticed himself to Dr. Benjamine Chandler of St. Albans, Vt. He was licensed to practice medicine by the "Third Medical Society of the State of Vermont, as established by law," in 1812.

War with England had been declared June 18, 1812, and Beaumont went to Plattsburg and presented his credentials to the authorities. Thus he began his long, colorful career as an army surgeon.

Beaumont's meeting with Alexis St. Martin, the subject of his experiments, took place June 6, 1822, when the retail store of the American Fur Company was crowded with Indians and voyageurs who were busy trading when a gun accidentally was discharged, with St. Martin the victim.

Beaumont describes the opening in the stomach as being as large as a man's fist. This cavity did not heal, although Beaumont wished to freshen the edge and close the opening with sutures. St. Martin would not consent to the operation.

The experiments were conducted by introducing food into the stomach through this orifice. Studies were made on various types of food, and digestion took place when the patient was in various states of anger, impatience, and fever. These experiments were the basis of modern gastric physiology.

It has been said that the opening was intentionally kept so, but authorities have proven this to be false. Beaumont supported St. Martin for several years on his salary of $40 per month.

In 1833, Beaumont decided to have his experiments published, and on July 29, he filed the title of his book with the clerk for the Southern District of New York. It was decided to sell the book for $3, but the records show that it was sold for only $2.

Beaumont died in St. Louis April 23, 1853. Alexis St. Martin, after deserting the care of Dr. Beaumont in 1834, died June 24, 1880, in Montreal.

Sir William Osler, who lived in Montreal at the time, took active measures to secure a necropsy, of at least the stomach, but was unsuccessful. The family resisted all requests, allowed the body to decompose, and had a grave dug eight feet below the surface to prevent any attempt at resurrection.

About the time this recent article appeared in the *Texas State Journal of Medicine,* an oil portrait of Dr. Beaumont was hung in the headquarters of the El Paso hospital for whom the Beaumont Army hospital was named.

Beaumont's monthly salary of $40 as a pioneer army surgeon in the wilderness of Wisconsin, indeed, did not insure a big financial gain for him; and generally in private practice throughout the country at that time the average doctor was very poor.

DOCTOR WILLIAM BEAUMONT
WHOSE DISCOVERIES BENEFITED THE WHOLE WORLD

PART II

TERRITORIAL WISCONSIN'S MEDICAL PIONEERS

Records show that some medical men in early territorial days were also serving as ministers of the gospel, holding Sunday worship services in private homes, barns, and schoolhouses, horsebacking from place to place.

In a few known cases, the work of physician was permanently abandoned and new pursuits were begun. In Sol Juneau's wilderness village of Milwaukee, for example, an in-migrant by the name of Frederick A. Luening centered his activities in the field of politics after quitting his medical practice elsewhere.

Just why Dr. Luening made this choice, no record shows. Maybe his medical fees had been insufficient to keep him out of debt. Perhaps he had been given little encouragement as a physician, knowing that, in most instances, when a patient was in great pain, straining the nerves in an effort to prevent death, the medicine of that day was of no practical value, with the death rate exceedingly high. In other words, too many sick persons were dying regularly while under the doctor's care.

Nevertheless, some learned men, with a fixed determination to make as many worthy contributions as possible to health, social, and spiritual enterprises, regardless of how great the hazards physically and financially, just kept serving in a dual capacity—medical and spiritual.

One of them was Rev. Cutting Marsh, a Congregationalist of Kaukauna, trained in both medicine and theology, who enjoyed being kind, helpful, and sympathetic while doing his best to lessen pain for the sick, giving testimony for God, showing unsaved persons how to be saved.

With some marked progress started in logging, lumbering, surveying, and lead mining in a region preparing

16

for territorial government of its own, the in-migration included strangers who, as sadly-inadequate, college-trained physicians, were carrying pungent medicine of their own make in wooden suitcases.

Fur Trader Sol Juneau, Father of Milwaukee, wasn't impressed by the handshake of any medical man unknown to him; and when his Indian wife became seriously ill one frigid winter night, he sent a trusted friend by the name of Fowler on a horseback trip over a snow-covered trail to Chicago, a marshland outpost of 300 or more people, a distance of 90 miles, to procure the right kind of medicine from a doctor friend.

Even though the doctor there did not know just what Mrs. Juneau's ailment really was, he gave the exhausted courier a remedy which, he felt, would get results.

Taking this remedy many days later, Sol's grateful wife responded in a way which indicated a definite cure. The medicine, she said, had been reliable.

What's your guess, dear reader, as to all the missing medical facts in this case? Can you set up a hypothesis, with all converging facts, showing Mrs. Juneau's evidence as unquestionably true?

According to a journal kept by one distinguished doctor of that day, medical charges were mostly for drugs, not medical service.

A most commonly known drug—a pill, called Compound Blue Mass—sold at the rate of four for 50 cents; and over a long period, one doctor prescribed it in 22 cases out of 94.

As to what ailment or ailments this pill was expected to help, the doctor did not record. His profit on each sale of four must have been in the pennies. His financial status must have been discouraging, since his income was chiefly from the non-wonder pills he could sell.

In retrospect now, reviewing the conditions under which sick people of that era really lived, looking back into what we now could rightfully term the *Very Sad Medical Age*, one easily understands the reasons why many strong men died early as the result of blood poisoning in a hand, arm, leg, or foot.

With germs unheard of and doctors unacquainted with the principles underlying the proper care of an infected wound, there was no control over the infecting organisms. Wounds actually were not given the right kind of treatment; they were not protected from further contamination and from added disability.

Antisepsis was unknown. So was anaesthesia. Chloroform, a potent, colorless, volatile, sweet-smelling fluid, with its many dangers, had not yet been discovered.

With superficial training, doctors had had no intense study of the normal physiological process. Their facilities were as inadequate as their knowledge. When evaluating an injured hand, they regarded it as an injury to a tendon or nerve. Not having been taught in a broad way, these men were not versed in the treatment of damage done to the underlying tendons, nerves, and other structures.

Imagine the extent of suffering for those persons who, with blood poisoning in hand or foot as the result of medical inefficiency, were permitted to die without any agency of relief.

Imagine also the agony suffered by an Indian fighter under Henry Dodge after being thrown from the back of a horse in battle, sustaining a fractured leg and having only some liquor as an ineffective pain reducer while watching an inexperienced surgeon work on his broken bones, vainly trying to put them together.

Yet the wounded warriors under Chief Black Hawk in 1832 didn't have anybody to offer help while dying at Pecatonica, Wisconsin Heights, and Bad Axe. Unattended, they just bled to death.

If Abraham Lincoln, 23, of New Salem, Illinois, had been seriously injured as a mounted officer of the volunteer Illinois militia, seeking to capture Black Hawk, his fight to live would have been frightful. Abe's chance of becoming President might have been effaced. He might not have been alive to free the slaves three decades later.

Minor surgery performed on young Lincoln then would have been unskilled, without anaesthesia, without asepsis and antisepsis. Any critical ailment, such as appendicitis, would have brought on sudden agony and death. Fate still was a terror for those whose abdominal pains were of the type unknown to medical doctors of that day.

Abe Lincoln's luck as a military man, however, was not wholly of the best, as shown on July 10, 1832—the time of his honorable discharge as a captain under General Atkinson near Lake Koshkonong, where a thief had stolen his horse, forcing him to return home by rowboat and by foot. For young Abe, transportation in Wisconsin was as primitive as medical science.

History being important and knowledge of the past throwing great light on developments of the future, there was a foundation on which influential men of medicine could build; and one of the real builders was Dr. Mason C. Darling of Fond du Lac, who was happy when learning that President Andrew Jackson had signed the bill which split up the Territory of Michigan and permitted the 20,000 or more persons in six huge counties west of Lake Michigan to establish a new territory of their own, called Wisconsin, which included Iowa and Minnesota, extending as far west as the Missouri River.

Darling, of far vision and courage, was eager to form a state society of doctors early in Wisconsin government; and at regular intervals, after Henry Dodge had been sworn in as the first governor, he made trips on horseback to the far-away hamlets of Milwaukee, Dodgeville, Belmont, Platteville, and Mineral Point to contact other astute medical pioneers and to affect the beginning of organized medicine in the new territory.

Madison's first family—the Eben Pecks—had not yet arrived; so Dr. Darling couldn't meet any fellow physician in that part of the wilderness.

The small band of crusaders who, with Darling, were showing a keen sense of duty, obviously were aware of the problems and the needs that were developing through the suddenly heavy influx of settlers along the rivers and lakes and in the area where lead ore was being mined.

Government land sales in 1836, in fact, had totaled 878,000 acres, priced at $1.00 and $1.25 per acre. Speculators had exhausted their savings in the purchase of land.

Strong men from Cornwall had been coming into the lead region, giving impetus to an activity which previously had been conducted chiefly by heavy drinkers of American birth. The average life span for them was to be short.

Approximately 1,000 men and women, residents of states bordering on Lakes Huron, Erie, and Ontario, had debarked from sailing vessels near the primitive Milwaukee shore within a short time, seeking boom opportunities and wealth.

Before this sudden inundation there, Indians outnumbered the white settlers, 200 to 120, in an environment of wigwams and log dwellings, moccasin-footed Indians, French-speaking fur traders, lonely transients, and a small colony of white in-migrants who had joined Sol Juneau in the big overall project of getting little Milwaukee under way as a place of great importance. Long lines of horses had been seen there ladened with costly peltries. At the request of Byron Kilbourn, founder of lasting enterprises in fields worthwhile, Dr. Increase A. Lapham had started to survey a townsite.

The wilderness was starting to undergo a big change. Medicine was not. Ambitions of frontiersmen were like the tide. Medical science was not working that way.

Government surveyors then were working along the Lake Michigan shore and the Fox-Wisconsin rivers. Unhappy Indians were beating their tom-toms for war.

Logging and lumbering was an industry well started as the result of the early initiative shown by John Shaw, native New Yorker and son of a Revolutionary War veteran, who, in his Black River operations, had become Wisconsin's first lumberman. Others who followed Shaw in this vital industry included Daniel Whitney, of New Hampshire, the first regular lumberman on the Upper Wisconsin river.

The small number of medical pioneers throughout the territory, therefore, was destined to meet a wide variety of new problems while seeking to improve the standards of both health and medicine. All challenges of a rapidly-changing, economic situation had to be met. General ethics among doctors had to be of the best, said modest Mason C. Darling and his associates as they sought to organize a strong medical society.

People at large had to be enlightened in the matter of improved sanitation. Also, a generally rough, frontier culture had to make way for a broadly objective behavior, so as to insure satisfactory territorial progress, these medical leaders said.

The process of education, unknown then in isolated Wisconsin, had to begin; and the doctors who were making known their dominant thoughts while horsebacking from one place to another, showing dignity, kindness, and self esteem, were in an ideal position from one day to the next. They easily could do much good in their contacts as a whole. Moreover, they had an opportunity to discover quackery in the field of medicine, and by banding together in opposition to medical impostors, they'd render a great public service.

Of course, in this Age of Pills, with nauseous and repulsive concoctions making sickness seem worse than it was, a self-sacrificing physician continued to be helpless each time a patient under his care was forced to die on a basis of just cruelty, with medical science not yet able to reduce the death rate considerably through timely, necessary discoveries. Yet this ineptness was not the family doctor's fault.

The doctor, in fact, could be no better than his college teachings—the extremely limited knowledge, experiences, training, and practices of the day.

Medical colleges, centered mostly in cultural Eastern states, were offering the best course that could be devised. Basic information, covering the history of world medicine, included the writings of all noted leaders of the past.

A student read the works of Paracelsus, German physician, who, in his lectures at the University of Basel years after the discovery of America by Columbus, mixed astronomy, superstition, necromancy, and occult philosophy together in what was termed the most logical theories and methods for use in treating disease. This overall teaching brought out the necessity for mineral baths. It made opium, mercury, and ore a part of pharmaceutics. Also, it made popular the use of tincture and alcoholic extracts.

Other sources of information included Hippocrates, of Asia Minor, referred to by critics as the father of medicine; and Thomas Sydenham, graduate of Oxford in the days of Cromwell and Charles I, founder of modern clinical medicine, who insisted upon accurate observations of disease as the real basis for medical practice, and whose brilliant accounts of malaria, plague, smallpox, hysteria, and gout contributed greatly to the advance of medical science.

Edward Jenner's conception of the importance of vaccination for smallpox was a topic for study, along with the material which was regarded by medical authorities of that day as pertinent to the course; and a student at graduation time was in possession of the knowledge which American medical doctors at large regarded as the best. Too, by his diploma, he was to adhere strictly to the approved standards of his profession.

So the pill doctors of Territorial Wisconsin who were advocating the formation of a society, assuredly, were doing the best they could with their limited medical knowledge. The men in this little group had strong faith. In all fields of endeavor, they could see better days ahead. Optimists they were when conditions were bad. They had initiative, loyalty, courage, and endurance. Horseback trips, made hazardous by snow and heavy rain, did not deter them from repeating those undertakings whenever the occasion required.

Yes, the founders of Wisconsin's medical profession were men of objectiveness and cheer. What they said and did was in the interest of better human relations. Readily adapting themselves to changing wilderness conditions, these men used sacrifice as a guide. All of them knew that, when aroused from sleep at night by a messenger who pounded at his log-house door, some person far off was critically sick, needing the quickest possible emergency help.

No storm could stop a territorial Wisconsin doctor from mounting a horse, with the aid of a candle or lantern light, then heading over an unsafe trail for the destination point to help bring a baby into the world.

Action was favorable and quick. Duty was regarded as a pleasure, not a sacrifice. The doctor's service, as his work and testimony revealed, was in accordance with the ideals which he had at the start of his practice, truly in keeping with the views on humaneness expressed by Hippocrates centuries before Christ.

A mother in agony, feeling that both she and her baby

would die, was not to be disappointed, even though destitute and unable to pay the doctor.

Fortunately for the gospel preachers of that day, they had medical doctors as influential aids in advocating a better way of life. For all of them, life was simple and quiet.

Small settlements were widely scattered. Only one wagon road had been built thus far. Called the military highway, it connected the three army garrisons of Crawford, Winnebago, and Howard.

River travel was via canoe. At times it was of exceptionally long duration, as evidenced by one trip made by a husband and wife from an Upper Wisconsin River location to the Illinois village of Chicago, where a stagecoach line was serving land travelers between that place and Ottawa.

If a doctor in the French settlement at Green Bay wished to serve a sick member of the Grignon family at Kaukauna, he had to travel either by horseback or canoe.

Travel was uncomfortable for a farm family in a hard-seated wagon drawn by two horses over a bumpy forest ground to the home of another family of settlers some miles away.

Vessels coming into that boom place controlled by 43-year-old Juneau and his affiliates were of masts and sails.

On that cold October day in 1836 at Belmont when our first territorial legislature was called into its first session by 54-year-old Henry Dodge, ex-Missouri sheriff, salt maker, miner, and planter, many of the 39 legislators who reported for roll call had traveled long distances on foot, with a pack containing items of vital use. At night they had slept on bare ground, with only a buffalo robe over them as a protection against freezing temperatures and wind. Others had come from far-away places on the back of a tired horse.

If any of these lawmakers had become seriously ill while enroute, suffering from abdominal pains, such as appendicitis or a ruptured bowel, they never would have seen the little wooden building in which Wisconsin government was to start. Bronchial-asthma would have destroyed them. Wolves would have devoured their lifeless bodies.

Nearly all of these $3.00 per day legislators, like the widely scattered men of medicine, who at times didn't average $3.00 per week, lived in log houses.

Gov. Dodge, prosperous lead miner, a resident of Dodgeville, far beyond the average span of life, drawing $2,500 from Congress as per-annum pay for his position as governor, who had won fame as a military man in torrent battle against savages, lived in a house fairly comparable to the prestige of an executive who was serving as both governor and superintendent of Indian affairs.

It was in this house, a short horseback ride from the temporary capitol at Belmont, where Gov. Dodge, during the first legislative session, had as his inspired guests John S. Horner of Virginia, the territorial secretary, whose annual salary was $1,200; Supreme Court Justice Charles Dunn, an in-migrant from Illinois, drawing what was considered a very big per-annum salary of $1,800; Marshal Francis Gehon, whose place of residence was Dubuque, Iowa; Territorial Attorney W. W. Chapman, resident of Burlington, Iowa; and others of high governmental rank.

As for the amount of pills needed by these men to keep well, there is no record. Some of them, particularly Judge Dunn, regarded liquor as a vital need of the day, surpassed in value by only beef. It was the right medicine for pain, for the restoration of lost energy, for resistance against shock and disappointment, some of the legislators insisted.

Drinkers here had to pay much more per glass and per gallon than those in the non-isolated states, where drunkenness was not as prevalent as in the frontier mining towns. In Massachusetts, where whiskey prices had dropped to an all-time low, one paid 25 cents per gallon. A cigar sold for a penny.

With no stagecoach service anywhere in the new Territory of Wisconsin, no pill-supply house to serve medical men, and the enterprising community of Chicago the closest point of contact, physicians in the sparsely settled Wisconsin localities did have a big supply problem.

In fact they had a wide variety of problems, including communication. Getting word from eastern states, for instance, in matters relating to the manufacture of a new drug or a newly developed medical technique was a process of extremely long delays, causing uncertainties and discouragement, which had to be offset by a higher degree of patience, tolerance, and hope.

Tragic, indeed, was a circumstance in which a doctor was out of pills, with his chief source of revenue cut off. A special trip overland from Mineral Point to Chicago and back was an undertaking which meant a time loss of several weeks as well as a heavy expense. Regardless of what route an unfortunate lead-region doctor would have been forced to take in his quest for urgent supplies in little Chicago, he was certain to meet many cruel challenges.

If, in his estimation, his travel route should be via horseback to far-off Ottawa in Illinois and thence via stagecoach eastward to his place of destination, his fortitude and courage had to be that of Nicolet, Doty, Dodge, or Marquette in order to succeed, especially if the trip was being made in near-zero weather. Also to complete such a trip successfully, the dutiful servant of the sick had to be physically strong. He couldn't afford to risk such hazards with a balky heart or other organ that was threatening to imperil him.

As a doctor of the wilderness, plying his profession far in advance of our so-called country doctor, that great exponent of sacrifice just had to rely greatly on his own knowledge, resources, and skill while living through the hardships of his time.

His status is well described in the *History of Dane County*, published by the late Albert O. Barton, distinguished and widely revered historian, who, as a vigorously working member of our State Historical Society, wrote as follows:

> Physicians were few and far between at the start of western settlement. Hence the first settlers, particularly those in the isolated farming districts, had to depend largely upon their own personal knowledge, abilities, and resources when sick or injured.
>
> As a rule, pioneers at large were wise in the lore of herbs, brews, and ointments, meeting ordinary situations and emergencies with much skill and success.
>
> Minor forms of surgery were resorted to by them, while extractions of teeth by farm forceps generally was common. In

Dane County, as elsewhere, necessity was the mother of invention.

The average death rate, steadfastly high, was in accordance with the enormous medical needs. It kept proving the apathy of science.

On that memorable day at Belmont in 1836, when Samuel C. Mazzuchelli, Roman Catholic priest of Sinsinawa, opened the first session of the territorial legislature with a prayer, emphasizing the principles of Christianity as of vital need in their process of voting and debate for a commonwealth as a whole, it was an era of inspiring progress in backwoods Wisconsin government, showing how determined leaders in law making, business, and industry could bring about marked improvements in their respective work fields while the world's best medical men were unable to announce any great discoveries in both surgery and drugs.

The germ theory of Louis Pasteur, French honor student and chemist, was in the offing, for Pasteur in that year of 1836 was a schoolboy of 13.

Antiseptic surgery, designed to eliminate bacteria in wounds, preventing putrefaction in compound fractures, also was of the distant future. Its discoverer, Joseph Lister, of England, was nine years old when Indian fighter Henry Dodge became Wisconsin's first chief executive. Three decades were to elapse before the principles of asepsis were to become known. Meanwhile, bacteria settled in wounds. Common were the deaths caused by gangrene. Hemorrhage in a wound frequently was most difficult to arrest.

Fortunately for Gov. Dodge, long a survivor of the roughest outdoor events, with extraordinary strength, fate generally was kind to him, preventing serious injury and keeping destructive germs out of his bloodstream. No medical butcher had an opportunity to work on him.

As one of Wisconsin's earliest white settlers, looking back upon a pageantry of exciting exploits, referring to the lead-mining industry as the most effective incentive for state growth, Dodge was in himself a potent population magnet. He and his fellow legislators were proving to the nation that Wisconsin, the old adventure land of painted Indians and rugged fur traders, had become the historic gateway of the West, gladly offering an environment of oxcarts and oxen,

"SHOCK-PROOF" ANDREW JACKSON when signing the bill which made Wisconsin a territory, was successfully defying bacilli. His appendix was not a death sentence. Dying at 78, he proved that, so far as his health was concerned, he was for nearly eight decades as invulnerable as his military attack at New Orleans.

crudely made wagons drawn by horses and mules, spinning wheels, candles, and candle molds, wooden spoons, rustic chairs, stone axes, arrowheads and spears, grog shops, prairie schooners, wigwams, feather headdress, Indian corn dances, disorders, and peace treaties, tent life for some people in summer, shanty life in winter.

Mineral Point had become known for its shaft cribbing, windlass, screening sieve, dog houses, and shanties. Gambling had become a prominent activity there. Government land sales had been brisk.

As a place of white habitation, Wausau was unknown, as were Eau Claire and Stevens Point; and in the far North, there was nothing to portend that townsites finally would be built at Rhinelander, Ashland, and Superior. Some cruisers even referred to the Upper Wisconsin River region as jungle land, unfit for habitation. For heavy hauling over roads of mud, farmers were using oxen.

John Jacob Astor, new baron of the fur trade, was pyramiding his riches through his enterprises at Prairie du Chien and Green Bay. Nobody in the wilderness of Wisconsin had a bath tub. Even in our nation's capitol, President Martin Van Buren didn't have one; and he, like our founding Wisconsin pioneers, had no gas, no electricity, no telephone or telegraph. Throughout the United States, there wasn't a public library. As for music, occasionally in Wisconsin a settler could be heard playing a fiddle. Like each government land sale, the tunes on a fiddle signified that our frontier had to go.

Not a single leader, including Gov. Dodge, was Wisconsin born. All members of the legislature were from places outside the territory. Some were from Ireland, others from 15 different states in our Union, including New Hampshire, Vermont, Rhode Island, Massachusetts, New York, and the Carolinas. Virtually it was a land of strangers, made up of strong men able to set the foundation for another great state prior to the discovery of germs and antisepsis, merciful anaesthesias, and surgery.

Surely, during that era of hardships and hazards, fate at times was kind to pioneers who, in their daily work, were in a struggle with adversity. For example, there wasn't a casualty or a disabling disease in July of 1837 when Augustus A. Bird and his 30 or more woodsmen-teamsters made that trip from Milwaukee to a new site called Madison for the purpose of constructing a capitol.

With wagon loads of machinery, stone-cutting tools, and other equipment obtained from eastern states, these men felled trees for many hours a day along a route not yet settled by a single person. In making a road, they removed stumps and brush, threaded through swamps, swam their horses across streams. They used trees as rafts in ferrying their wagons, machinery, equipment, and supplies. They fought rainstorms, slept in the open at night. In 10 days they reached the destination place triumphantly, all of them. History it was in pageantry style. As a lasting testament of frontier-Wisconsin progress, it was a story of mighty men striding the stage, their physiques successfully defying the weaknesses of medical science, the severity of daily life, the threats of disaster caused by injury and destructive germs.

Epic-like characters were among Contractor Bird's work force on that site called Madison, and one of them was Darwin Clark, a New Yorker, age 21, who, while reading an advertisement in his home-town paper concerning the big Wisconsin boom, decided to take part in it.

He had enough money to make a trip on water to sprouting Detroit. There he began a hazardous trip on foot, crossing Michigan from east to west, thence through that part of Indiana which led to the old Illinois fort established by Henry Dearborn, former Secretary of War.

From this place in Chicago, young Clark headed northward to Milwaukee, following the shore. Hungry and tired, he finally got his feet wet while fording a stream between Milwaukee and Madison. Near a bonfire at night, while drying out his shoes, he fell asleep. Upon awakening the next morning, he found that his shoes had been burned. Then, from a knapsack he took some cloth, tore it into two pieces and wrapped each piece around a foot, so as to be able to complete his journey without shoes.

Without injury or sickness, this boy had been blessed real good. He was given a job as a carpenter at the little mill site located near Lake Mendota at Madison soon after the capitol-building project got under way. He was not worn out as the result of his adverse-walking experiences for a distance of approximately 500 miles through a wilderness trail which had a very small number of settlements, widely scattered.

The capitol completed after many long delays caused by the primitive-transportation factor, the national panic, and the acute shortage of material that was coming from manufacturing centers of the East, there finally was a growing community, with legislators contributing greatly to the gradual population increase.

Little Madison then needed a medical doctor. In short time there was a physician named Almon Lull staying at the newly built American House, ready to help the sick.

Dr. Lull was one of the guests who slept in a room six feet square. The partition between him and the stranger in the next room was a blanket which hung from the ceiling.

In winter, it was cold there, with a small stove of ancient make feebly trying to furnish warmth; but the hotel as a whole was not quite as frigid as the interior of the little wooden capitol which stood on a pretty-looking square across the street. There the floor boards, made from lumber that had not been dried after the sawing process, were covered with ice in spite of a heated stove. So were the seats when legislators were not sitting on them.

No doubt the poor Dr. Lull, when forming acquaintances, saw the disturbed Ebenezer Childs of Brown County going into the open basement to poke pigs with a long pole, making them squeal loud enough to break up noisy debates in the legislature upstairs.

It wasn't long before a medical man of true eminence was taking part in these historic debates. His name was Mason C. Darling, the first physician of Fond du Lac, who in time was to see service as presiding officer in both houses, later going to congress.

Meanwhile, he was the leader of that movement which, in 1841, resulted in the formation of the State Medical Society. Linked with his name in the act which became law were Doctors Bushnell B. Cary, Lucius I. Barber, Oliver E. Strong, Edward McSherry, E. W. Wolcott, J. C. Mills, David Walker, Horace White, Jonas P. Russell, David Ward, Jesse S. Hewett, and B. O. Miller.

All of these doctors, in proving that the medical profession was to make progress in keeping with the development of their territory, were then being seriously affected by the adverse economical conditions which had grown out of the Panic of '37.

People generally were getting deeper in debt, and the hazards of credit were becoming extremely difficult for even the kind merchants to endure. Milwaukeeans paid $25 a barrel for flour, $15 for a bushel of potatoes, shipped from Buffalo, N. Y.

The first bank had quit business. Chartered in '35 by the territorial legislature of Michigan, it had been headed originally by land speculator and former jurist Morgan L. Martin of Green Bay, cousin of Judge Doty, one of the building commissioners of the new territory. Martin's connection with this bank had not been long. He did not like the banking conditions of that day.

Notes valued at $182,000 were on the books, with a mass of valueless securities and an unlimited amount of worthless paper afloat when the defunct bank closed its doors. Editors of the Milwaukee and Green Bay weekly newspapers finally were reporting that wildcat banks throughout the nation had not had enough gold and silver available to redeem their notes.

Long-delayed news reaching Milwaukee from the East kept pointing out that employment generally was in a crisis, with nine-tenths of the nation's factory workers thrown into idleness. At New York and Philadelphia, reports said, starving men had been breaking into warehouses for flour. The whole economic system had collapsed. Deficiency diseases were on the increase.

Pill Doctor Enoch Chase, Milwaukee, like all other men of medicine, was reporting the low morale of sick people on his list. In the legislature daily there were loud denunciations of fraud in government; and a chief exponent of harsh words then was William S. Hamilton, son of the illustrious Alexander Hamilton, George Washington's secretary of the treasury.

A resident of Wiota, Hamilton had been in the territory since the days before the birth of industry. His coming here was the outgrowth of an experience in which he drove a herd of cattle all the way from Springfield, Ill., to Fort Howard at Green Bay.

While Hamilton was blasting the agents of fraud, impoverished medical doctors were serving penniless people who were sick. Gospel preachers, themselves without funds and proper food, were buying feed for their horses on a basis of long credit and were making trips by horseback from one distant place to another in the same manner as of old.

Undaunted by this awful panic, ministers were furnishing groggy Wisconsin with a spirit that was to lead its distressed people out of the dark. Among them were Jackson Kemper, Episcopal bishop and founder of the Nashota House; Alfred Brunson, Methodist, of the lead region; Richard Cadle, Duck Creek, superintendent of the Oneida Indian school, living near the blazed-trail route which connected Chicago with Green Bay; Father Samuel C. Mazzuchelli, Catholic priest of Sinsinawa; Bishop Baraga, Village of LaPointe; Salmon Stebbins, Protestant of Milwaukee, whose first Sunday sermon at Madison was in a saloon; and Sherman Hall, eminent missionary among Indians, who finally was in the LaPointe area.

By this time, quackery had become a disgusting national evil, so much so that the medical society in the state of Texas had started a war on it. In the big cities of our country, the trail of quackery had been long, especially in the field of drugs. One fake advertiser said his drug was a cure for cancer. Other advertisers had water and steam cures. According to an advertisement in one weekly newspaper, a patent medicine was a real cure for rupture. Drugs sold during that era were not inspected and analyzed by chemists. Government control was unheard of. Impure drugs were not confiscated and destroyed.

Members of the newly formed State Medical Society of Wisconsin were discussing this pungent condition at their meeting places. Soon a quorum agreed that immediate action was necessary in urging Congress to enact a pure-drug law which would eliminate quackery. The New York College of Pharmacy, in fact, had already recommended it.

PART III

STATEHOOD AND WHAT THE DOCTORS WERE DOING

In 1848, with the citizenry set for statehood, one of the prominent delegates at the constitutional convention was Dr. Alfred L. Castleman, 40-year-old resident of Delafield, whose boyhood was spent in Kentucky.

An untiring organizer, spearheading movements which the onrushing Wisconsin government needed in the field of health, Castleman fought for the establishment of a mental hospital. At each meeting of the State Medical Society, he also urged the raising of medical standards. He was the Society's third president and for a long time was on the University of Wisconsin Board of Regents.

Preceding Castleman as head of the medical organization was Dr. J. B. Dousman, Milwaukee, who, in 1848, put through a resolution which asked Congress to protect the public against impure drugs. Recommended by him and his colleagues was Federal inspection of all chemical substances intended to cure the sick. Discovery of adulterated substances was to be followed by quick confiscation and destruction.

The next year, when the California gold rush lured Hamilton and other great Wisconsinites away from their habitats, the crusading doctors of early statehood were achieving new goals. One objective was to establish a University of Wisconsin medical school. Another was to put more potency in the war against quackery. As an incentive to strengthen State Medical Society membership, the legislative body adopted a standing rule requiring in-migrant doctors to prove their qualifications by way of a test in order to become members.

Marked progress was on the way. Dentists were using gas. They introduced ether in extracting teeth. They were making dentistry an attractive profession. In the city of Milwaukee, with a population of 9,500, compared with Madison's 600, dentists were among the foremost civic leaders.

It was the start of the stagecoach era. No longer was mail being carried afoot between Chicago and Green Bay. In retrospect were the hardships of Moses Hardwick and Alexis Clermont, who, in early periods of wilderness history, made the 200-mile trip by foot, carrying 60 pounds of mail on their rock-like shoulders.

The stagecoach line between Milwaukee and Madison was an aid for doctors who, as members of the State Medical Society's legislative committee, were required to contact legislators within the capitol in matters relating to improved public health.

A telegraph line between Milwaukee and Madison now insured a timely newspaper service. Horse-and-buggy travel was on the increase. Banks were still reflecting the effects of that dreadful panic. Public servants were poorly paid. In Milwaukee the yearly pay for a schoolteacher was not indicative of the value of education. Male teachers there received $400. Women got one-half of that amount.

The Milwaukee Public Health Department had begun to put lime in streets and alleys as a prevention against disease. Pigs, as well as unharnessed horses, were moving up and down the alleys daily. Policemen were carrying poisoned meat in coat pockets and feeding it to stray dogs in order to enforce a city ordinance.

The State Medical Society was advocating a law requiring that lye be labeled as poison. Housewives were using lye for cleaning purposes. Doctors were saying that children might swallow some lye.

Statehood under Nelson Dewey and his immediate successors had brought forth some noteworthy progress, and when roads were being made from planks, not only the farmers derived great benefits but the men of medicine who rode over them.

State Medical Society leaders, in conference with J. H. Lathrop, LL.D., University of Wisconsin chancellor, regarding the establishment of a medical school, emphasized the need for earliest possible action. A high code of ethics was a topic regularly listed on the Society's agenda.

Came the formation of the Dane County Medical Society under C. P. Chapman. Similar action was taken in nearby counties.

Wisconsin physicians everywhere were saying they wanted honest statements on all labels pasted on bottles containing medicine. Quack manufacturers were continuing to make their products flow into the drug market.

Deficiency diseases, broadened in scope as a result of the disgusting food situation—aftermath of the panic—had brought on much sickness, loss of employment, shattered credit.

Throughout this period of transition, Doctors Darling, Fond du Lac; Dousman, Milwaukee; Castleman, Delafield; and Van Dusen, Mineral Point, were making most effective contributions for the people of their state. What they were doing together was truly symbolic of greatness at its best.

People of Milwaukee, without cows, chickens, and pigs, who had been weakened by undernourishment and hunger in early territorial days as a result of the panic, finally were hit hard by fever, which brought on complications and many deaths.

As of yore, the most common of epidemics were fought with ineffective drugs. Persons critically ill were in confinement at home, not in a hospital, for medical science still was in its wilderness stage of progress.

Anyone stranded by deep snowdrifts, showing signs of a direct threat of pneumonia, really was in a struggle to survive, and when forced into a crudely made bed in a drafty log house or shanty, with a high fever, exhaustion and pain, under the care of a medical doctor who was of little help, the physical outlook was of the worst. Lungs and heart soon were disabled. Energy was imperiled, nerves worn away, and general resistance made feeble. The patient's reliance on medicine for a cure was soon abandoned.

People who continuously withstood all challenges of germ, storm, undernourishment, and plague, avoiding serious illness, actually were not experiencing the fear and disappointments which a very weak medical profession was helping to create among the sick.

Truly fortunate were those Easterners who were able to work their way through severe hardships and storm when reaching isolated Chicago in their trek to that little place of opportunity and grim reality called Milwaukee during the early land boom.

Hauling their most valuable belongings on heavy sleds over Lake Michigan ice and along a shore which had no house, shed, or barn as a sleeping place, these seekers of Wisconsin fortune defied all threats of adversity and disease. Then, while adjusting themselves sensibly to changing frontier conditions, they saw a frail medical profession using faulty experiments and nauseous, ineffective remedies when battling that dreaded epidemic called cholera.

Yet the average Milwaukeean of that era—the 1840s—was in a high state of optimism and tolerance; and local history was mostly fun for Willie Sivyer and other boys of the East Side, who rolled barrels of New York flour from a grocery store to home, killed wild pigeons with clubs in helping to provide family food, swam their cows across river daily from pasture to home at milking time.

Their milk, of course, wasn't pasteurized—a process then unknown; and cows infected with the germ of tuberculosis actually were giving it to persons who drank their white fluid.

During the cold-weather months, some of the cow owners had a problem in seeking to provide suitable shelters for them in order to prevent pneumonia and to insure a strong resistance against sub-freezing temperatures, which followed every heavy snowfall.

The rate of tuberculosis in territorial Wisconsin at that time was on the increase, with science unable to combat it successfully. Major diseases in dairy herds were not eliminated. Dangerous microorganisms, originating in the cow, were steadily permitted to contaminate the milk. Healthy citizens, as a result, became victims of the Great White Plague. Of the cheerful news items during early territorial years concerning the value of new discoveries, the one relating to the love apple cheered the growers of vegetables, who previously had shunned it, saying it was poison.

This love apple, to become known as the tomato—an excellent source of nutrition—eaten in Europe as early as the 16th century, was not appearing as food in Wisconsin until many years after Henry Dodge's first term as governor. By that time, saws were buzzing in 125 different logging areas. The mail route between Milwaukee and Madison had been changed from weekly to semi-weekly. Wisconsin had been producing nearly one half of the nation's lead ore. Friends of Bill Caffee in the lead region had created widespread talk by massaging Caffee's chest while trying to restore life after he had been hanged for murder.

In this generation, like the others which preceded it, the average person everywhere wasn't getting enough help from the medical profession to warrant a long span of life. Proof was in the doctor's office, in mortuary, in graveyard.

Surgery was cruel; and with germs, asepsis, and antisepsis not yet known, people who experienced painful operations actually were being tortured.

As told by Dr. William Edwin Ground of Superior, renowned surgeon, who headed the State Medical Society:

> "It is easy to vision the horrors of surgery in the pre-anaesthetic days, when the operating room must have resembled something between a torture chamber and a slaughter house — a sight which was calculated to bring a feeling of revulsion to any but the most callous."

Fortunately for this country and for Carl Schurz, the German-born celebrity did not have to undergo an operation of this kind after settling in Watertown to help his wife Margarethe start Wisconsin's first kindergarten and to otherwise make great personal history for himself through politics, government, and war service.

As for the status of those who at that time were serving as medical doctors, Cornelius A. Harper described it lucidly and adequately when, as State Health Officer, he said:

> Those physicians were varied in training, type, and objectives. All practiced as best they could. The variability of their training in Wisconsin was common to nearly all the states, probably more ap-

plicable to the Midwest and Far West than in the more established settlements of our East. Some of these men had academic training in college. Others had little academic work prior to their taking up the study of medicine here. They entered the profession with a lack of training and experience.

This condition was merely characteristic of the times. Few reasonably-standardized colleges existed in this country. Moreover, there were colleges in which the study term was short. Diplomas were obtained easily after a few months of attendance. These schools of learning were called diploma mills.

According to the stock of drugs kept by the New York College of Pharmacy in those days when Medical Society members everywhere were seeking a national Pure Drug law, following are some of the drugs being sold: quinine, cough mixture, calomel, Ipecac, and Citrini Ungt., the last item of which was prescribed for the itch. One of its most noted users, a Texas doctor said in a journal kept by him, was the last vice-president of the Republic of Texas.

Other drugs of that period, sold by doctors everywhere, included Dovers powders, paregoric, equivater, nitro-muriatic acid, calc. magnesia, hartshorne, elix. vitriol, tart, bitters, morphine, corrosive sublimate, antacid mixture, carbonate potash, emetic, sal rochelle, sulphur ppt., squill pills, myrrh, balsam, cantharides, febrifuge pulvules, iodine, ergot, lobelia, tartar potash, tartar emetic, camphor, cooks' pills, laudanum, astringent pills, anti-dysenteric mixture, compound blue mass.

All were legitimate drugs, outside of the "Cure Cancer and All Else" concoctions which fake manufacturers were advertising in newspapers of the country.

From this list, the medical doctors of Milwaukee picked what was most appropriate when treating patients for cholera in 1849—year of the ruinous Milwaukee plague, when 104 persons died within the first month, adding shocks to a population that was living through bank and church riots, damaging labor disorders, reports of shipwrecks, jailbreaks, and endless political chicanery.

So frightened was the population at large that the city marshal did not permit the appearance of even one mud puddle within the city limits. Workers under him drained hundreds of stagnant puddles. They carried 1,000 or more wagon loads of rotted vegetation and refuse to the dumping ground outside the city.

Fortunately for Ole Bull, famed 39-year-old Norwegian violinist, he wasn't in this area when the plague was in its rage. His Wisconsin timing was of the best.

Hundreds of German immigrants were not that lucky.

The so-called hospitals of the day were merely pest houses, or place of last resort for persons who were getting ready to die.

A Protestant minister by the name of William Passavant became operator of a pesthouse which eventually, as the Milwaukee Hospital, not only was the first Protestant institution of its kind in the United States but a pioneering hospital organization which did much to develop hospital efficiency in this state.

The start of a great era it was, with Levi Booth and Charles Wakely becoming widely known as the first University of Wisconsin graduates, 38 counties reporting the establishment of a school system, the Milwaukee and Mississippi Railroad Company giving Wisconsin its first train on rails, which extended from Milwaukee to Prairie du Chien; and Lyman Copeland Draper of New York State trudging along primitive farm roads, with a knapsack of diaries, journals, and notebooks hanging from his thin shoulders as he ferreted out personal history by visiting pioneers, obtaining original documents and otherwise doing those things which in time were to build the State Historical Society's library into a mammoth department of records.

It was a period of turbulent political wars, with Gov. Barstow and his party legislators at Madison continually referred to as scoundrels by the editors of some newspapers. Madison's chief satirist, when challenging Milwaukee's Rufus King, was giving his newspaper a public-nuisance rating. Vulgarity had become a weapon. Farmers of Dane County, after seeing Barnum's menagerie, kept saying they had been deceived. A colony of Swiss had begun to make New Glarus a prominent cheese-making place. Milwaukee's German population kept increasing in a big way. It was a factor in raising the population of Wisconsin from 30,945 in 1840 to 305,530 in 1850. Political candidates were called Barn Burners, Loco-Focos, Free Soilers, and Know-Nothings.

John Deere had made pioneer farmers happy with his plow invention. Wisconsin marble had been shipped to the nation's capital for use in erecting a monument in memory of George Washington. Gas lamps, first seen on Milwaukee streets, were to become of great importance in city improvement everywhere. Indians of the North were being hit appallingly by smallpox. When logs were being rafted, the St. Croix and Upper Wisconsin rivers were so jammed that very little flowing water could be seen. New villages kept springing up in the central part of the state. People of West Bend, with 35 store buildings, now had a carpenter and tin shop, a grist mill, some blacksmiths, a hardware, grocery, drug and shoe store, a brick yard, lime kiln, and two breweries.

In Milwaukee, anti-slavery speeches were becoming hotter every week. Shot Tower at Helena had become nationally known. Stephen Foster's *Oh, Susanna!* generally was the most popular song. Steam-propelled vessels had become common. Progress in navigation had been one of the factors denoting Wisconsin's onward march. In the dim past now was that event of 1841 when a small steam-engine craft from Buffalo, with a paddle wheel astern and a smoke-pipe in center, came into a Milwaukee wharf. When at full speed, it amazingly made 10 miles per hour.

Since that time the cavalcade of history had brought forth many steam-vessel improvements.

A medical doctor now in Milwaukee or Madison, when in dire need of drugs, could send a telegram to a supply house in Chicago and, within a short time, receive his order in the mail.

Another encouraging fact for him was that, if he were a passenger on a train entering the Milwaukee railroad station, he immediately could step onto an omnibus operated by Dad Davis and be taken to his favorite hotel. The bus, handsomely painted in buff, with light blue panels all garnished with intricate scrollwork, stopped at every hotel in town.

Nevertheless, for all those who rode on this omnibus and for everyone else residing in or outside the state, the pills prescribed by medical men were still bitter and too often ineffective.

Official statistics showed that, for every 617 persons in the United States, there was one medical doctor.

No doubt these figures included an adventurer from Maine—Edwin Ellis, an 1844 graduate of Bowdoin College, who followed in the wake of Henry Longfellow, Nathaniel Hawthorne, and Franklin Pierce.

From a standpoint of courage, fortitude, and numerous other virtues, including a determination to achieve his objective ends—conquering the wilderness, helping to set up a permanent community in the most isolated part of the state, serving as a unique public servant in the fields of education, medicine, banking, and culture, this man really proved to be the father of town builders in Upper Wisconsin.

Starting from an outpost called Saint Paul, Minn., during the winter of 1855-56, with snowstorms making foot travel hazardous over old Indian trails, the 32-year-old Doctor Ellis walked alone to the extreme western end of Lake Superior on snowshoes and then followed the south shore to a point just opposite LaPointe on the island of Madeline, with its Indian population of approximately 500, connected to the mainland by thick ice.

The doctor was headed for Chequamegon Bay, the place at which Father Allouez had set up Wisconsin's first log chapel, the site where the French fur traders Radisson and Grosielliers had established Wisconsin's first white habitation two centuries before.

A careful study of the map for that region had caused Doc Ellis to regard Chequamegon as an ideal place for development; and when reaching the head of the bay there, he met a heavily-bearded frontiersman by the name of Asaph Whittlesey, who already had cultivated the same thought. Whittlesey, in fact, had felled many trees, had made some lumber in his own crude way and had built a house, preparatory to making that place his future home.

Later, as a member of the legislature, Whittlesey was going to the capitol at Madison all the way by foot, sleeping on the ground, with a bonfire to keep the wolves away, relying on his reserve strength to offset the rigors of hunger.

Could you make one trip like that and avoid collapse?

As to whether Dr. Ellis did or did not have a small satchel of pills with him upon arrival there, records do not show; but he did administer to the sick as the embryo town of Ashland was in the building stage. He was a dominant force in the development of a school system, a bank, a library, and many industrial enterprises.

What courage! What initiative! What a man!

For many years the closest settlement of any note was at Wausau, far on the Southeast, with a population of about 450, a solid forest between that place and Ashland, and only some blazed Indian trails, some lakes, and some streams as routes of travel.

The State Medical Society, headed by Dr. John Mitchell of Janesville, then was asking the legislature to build a hospital for the insane. Other news of that day concerned Laura J. Ross, a New Englander, who had become Milwaukee's first woman doctor.

In 1857, when Robert M. LaFollette was two years old, and the first box bed spring in the United States was imported from France, Dr. D. Cooper Ayres of Green Bay and others of the State Medical Society were discussing the startling discovery of Louis Pasteur, 35-year-old French chemist, who had clarified the phenomenon of fermentation.

For the first time in world history, medical men were acquiring knowledge concerning germs. They were getting ready to do what all of the physicians of the troubled past were unable to do—learn how to fight life's dominant killers, known as the disease-producing bacilli.

Pasteur, in his discovery, showed that putrefaction is due to microbes coming from the air. His proven experiments disclosed the old fallacies concerning the phenomenon of fermentation. Now it was found that milk could be soured by injecting a number of organisms from buttermilk or beer kept unchanged if similar organisms were excluded.

"The chemical act of fermentation," Pasteur said, "is essentially a correlative phenomenon of a vital act beginning and ending with it."

Virtually, Pasteur's germ theory was leading the meagerly trained medics out of the woods. Some men hailed it as the greatest discovery in world history. As a result of its growing benefits, life expectancy in this country was to be most encouraging—a key factor in making America strong. Certainly it was a stark reminder of the onslaughts which tiny microorganisms had made on man continuously since the start of time.

Because of Pasteur, the history of disease and death was to undergo a vast change. Life generally was to offer a much better outlook, with England's Joseph Lister destined to exploit Pasteur's germ theory and to introduce his antiseptic surgery—the greatest of all gifts to the surgeons of this world. In due time a compound fracture no longer would be regarded as a death sentence. The percentage of babies dying at birth was to be reduced considerably. During early statehood, one-half of the babies died at birth.

In 1857, when the subject of slavery was an explosive issue everywhere, with cholera the most persistent health threat in Wisconsin towns, members of the State Medical Society were recording case histories. Diplomas, signifying the successful completion of the Society's entrance test, were given to new members. The state legislature was considering a proposal that a Bureau of Vital Statistics be set up. A surgeon, during a Medical Society meeting, displayed a chloroform mask which, he said, was being used by London's illustrious Doctor Lister. He told about Lister's lectures on surgery at the Royal infirmary. A discussion later concerned the use of anaesthesia.

This was the first mention of anaesthesia in the state society's records; and in meetings that followed, there was much comment concerning the use of chloroform and its effects.

Manufactured by chlorination of alcohol or acetone in an alkaline solution, the anaesthesia called chloroform became known for its dangers. Extremely potent, it was being dropped upon an open mask by a surgeon at the start of an operation. Another technique was in blowing this vapor into the patient's airway.

When an overdosage was a reality, there was some damage to the patient's heart and to his or her liver. Blood pressure was known to fall. Because of these facts, members of the State Medical Society were emphasizing the need for highest efficiency when using that clear, sweet-smelling fluid which had a burning taste, called chloroform.

Even when used properly in those early days of anaesthesia and vast uncertainty, chloroform was not assurance that a man would live after the amputation of a leg. In most cases, an amputation meant death. A compound fracture was a frightening mortality hazard.

Until England's Joseph Lister could introduce his antiseptic principles to surgery, applying undiluted carbolic acid upon a compound fracture, an operation of this kind was one of grave danger.

Yet, in spite of this knowledge, some men permitted recklessness to lead them into unnecessary trouble, disability, and broken bones. For example, at Port Washington in 1862, after conscription had been put into effect, rioters of foreign birth risked fatal bodily injury by storming the courthouse with clubs, smashing windows and doors, destroying documents, and otherwise inciting counter action which meant bone breaking, bloodshed, and pain.

The odds were heavily against these mobsters at the start, for serious injury often was stalked by death.

In 1860, when settlers at Portage had no wells, used melted snow for drinking and cooking purposes, built fences out of sod and soil; when Wisconsin's wheat production gained nation-wide publicity, with its 28-million bushels; when Abe Lincoln's popular vote throughout the Great Lakes region was solid; when Milwaukee was best known for its torrid action in behalf of Joshua Glover, a fugitive slave, who started a Wisconsin war, the medical world was still waiting for Dr. Lister in his university chair of surgery at Glasgow to make known his carbolic-acid experiments. Lister's work on the coagulation of blood, a subject related to the early stages of inflammation, already had received the plaudits of surgeons here.

At that time in Wisconsin, when cholera was a recurrent-health destroyer, the lack of an effective drug was causing the victims of cholera to concoct all sorts of chemical mixtures. A gospel preacher said he had found a cure —a teaspoonful of powdered charcoal, taken three or four times a week in a cup of coffee or tea. Another helpful remedy, he reported, was a mixture of laudanum, brandy, and charcoal, to be taken at intervals of five minutes.

A Milwaukee editor, who printed this medicinal item, later did not mention whether these concoctions had become popular. Surely the cost was small, and a dollar in those days satisfied many wants. Room and board at Milwaukee's Female Seminary, for example, was at the rate of $2.00 per week. The cost of washing there weekly was 25 cents. Education was not expensive in a city already known for its beer. Optimists, when bragging, did not forget that Milwaukee was much bigger than the nation's capital. A fellow, when courting his girl friend, could do well with a dollar in his pocket. Stick candy was a nickel a pound.

In that century, as well as now, a person could not fully trust the stomach. He or she could not tell what all was taking place within the kidneys, the liver, the heart, the tonsils, the lungs. Woe unto them whose organs were causing acute trouble, giving the medical experimenters an opportunity to torture them.

Of course, many of these citizens were fortunate, reaching the age of 60, 70, or 80 without any physical impairment; but on a basis of the medical inefficiency of the day, the history of painful surgery and heavy death toll, the feeling of uncertainty and fear was generally known to be strong. Well advised persons were aware that faithful, dignified surgeons were operating on parts they knew little or nothing about, arguing with fellow members of a state association as to just what was what in the field of the guess. A prominent 1860 doctor in Texas once got into a hot controversy concerning newfangled homopathy, which, in the estimation of other doctors, was a proper treatment for scabies. The following is what he said:

"In reality, if like is cured by like, the internal administration of louse tea should cure the itch."

The speaker was in a society which, based on its unusual accomplishments, was making Texas one of the nation's foremost medical leaders.

A daily newspaper story from that part of the country pointed out the first successful operation on the tongue for cancer. News of this kind kept encouraging Wisconsin surgeons, who needed all the authentic information they could obtain in order to improve their techniques.

In April, 1861, when Gov. Randall was calling for a volunteer regiment at the start of war between our states, the youngsters who enlisted were to suffer terribly from the effects of a surgeon's knife as well as enemy gunfire.

The legs of many were to be sawed off, because of improper treatment of fractures, with surgeons lacking the knowledge of asepsis and antisepsis, not applying undiluted carbolic acid to any fracture, not knowing how to arrest a hemorrhage in aseptic wounds, using silk or flax when tying an artery, the long ends being left, so as to insure the escape of pus.

In that war, wounded men had microbes to fight along with their pains. Microbes, settling on a thread, caused suppuration. These microorganisms became imbedded among the tissues of a wound. Surgeons, not having heard of them, did not know they were there.

Often, before an operation beyond a line of fire, a surgeon did not scrub and rinse his hands in soap and water, not having the time to do so as a result of emergency. Yet, in his regrets, the underfed, weary, army surgeon was learning much concerning all types of injuries and wounds. He had an opportunity to improve his own surgical techniques. In time, all of the newly acquired knowledge and experiences were certain to benefit the long, groping, medical profession.

Most horrible in retrospect was the history of disease, pollution, hunger, agony, and death at Andersonville and Libby prisons.

During that war, activities of the State Medical Society of Wisconsin were suspended. Many of the members were in service, and because of the heavily increased demands that were made upon those doctors who remained at home, medical meetings were not held.

Through the American Medical Association, beneficial news was funneled to state associations. One great discovery followed another.

A child on a boarding-house bed, suffering from a tumor, was saved from death and was able to grow into motherhood when a surgeon of exceptional skill in an outside state performed an operation called ovariotomy.

This report was just another in that series which in time would place surgery on a plane high enough to warrant strong public acclaim.

In the successful operation for ovariotomy, the surgeon said the pedicle had been tied off and returned—an extraordinary procedure. They then were treated extraperitonially. The diagnosis was accurately made. The removed tumor was a unilocular cystoma, the size of an adult's head.

At a time when there was no defined method of operation in our country at large, one Texas surgeon performed something startling—a hysterectomy. Broad ligaments were tied off with silk, piece-meal, the surgeon using for this purpose an aneurism needle.

Currently an operation of this kind—removal of the uterus from the body by excision—is commonly successful surgery.

With the establishment of antiseptic surgery by England's Doctor Lister, medical men everywhere were to become known as true agents of mercy. In the past, many of them had been referred to as butchers.

Proof of the bacterial cause of disease by Pasteur had opened a new horizon in problems of public health.

In 1865, when the cities of Madison and Fond du Lac were pressing each other for the distinction of being Wisconsin's second largest population center, both credited with approximately 10,000 inhabitants, as compared with Milwaukee's 49,000, Dr. Lister was applying undiluted carbolic acid to a compound fracture. Because of his successes, physicians everywhere were learning how to arrest a hemorrhage in aseptic wounds. Formerly it was a practice to use silk or flax when tying arteries, the long ends being left to provide the escape of pus.

In the development of this new surgical technique, the objective was to eliminate the old hazard resulting from microbes settling on a thread and causing suppuration. Microbes formerly had an opportunity to become embedded among the tissues of a wound. Experiments led to eventual use of a sulphochronic catgut.

It was Dr. Lister who vigorously pointed out that the public's greatest health danger was in the air. It was Lister who introduced carbolic acid for use in surgery.

In years immediately following the war between North and South, the State Medical Society of Wisconsin was adding much impetus to its activity in public-health improvement. In one instance it was asking the legislature to spend money for the education of the blind. Care of imbeciles, too, was a matter placed before the legislature. Pressure was put on University of Wisconsin officials to establish a medical school. Fraud was being fought.

In 1867, when burly men of the woods, employed by Isaac Stephenson of Marinette, had placed five million feet of logs into the Menominee River and rafted them millward in what had become a boom industry in that part of the state; when hop culture was a popular subject for daily-newspaper editors; when shipyard officials at Manitowoc proudly announced that 30 vessels, with a tonnage of 8,158, had been built by them thus far at a cost of $512,000; when Pony Express riders, on their first trip between Missouri and the Pacific Coast, covered the distance in 10 days to amaze the general public; when war veterans were supporting short, blue-eyed, General Grant for the presidency; when hardened loggers from Maine were taking part in Wisconsin's timber onslaught; when songs of Stephen Foster no longer were selling well in Milwaukee; when electric lights and telephones were still unknown, the State Medical Society was strengthening its efforts to advance medical education. Each member pledged his personal help in getting vital bills passed in the legislature.

At the same time, a Milwaukee doctor by the name of Laura Ross was a dynamic force in the struggle for woman suffrage. She and Lila Peckham were organizing lecture tours and fiery state conventions. Through them, suffrage was getting ahead. Susan B. Anthony, the nation's chief crusader, accepted their invitation to speak.

Tuberculosis, uncontrolled and steadily increasing through contaminated milk and through germ-spreading conditions in public places and in homes, was a dangerous health threat in many localities.

Two years later, in 1869, a committee from the State Medical Society urged the legislature to repeal the charter that had been granted to a Milwaukee agency—referred to as a fake institution of learning, engaged in the sale of diplomas.

With the logging and lumber industry gradually reaching gigantic proportions, physicians in those areas were confronted with many new problems of surgery. The types of injury were numerous, ranging from fractures to ugly cuts. With limited or little knowledge concerning major surgery, these doctors suddenly found themselves working on broken hips, pelves, vertebrae, brain, necks, kneecaps, eyes, noses, arms, ribs, and legs. Uncertainty had to be offset by faith, poise, and perseverance as each self-taught, backwoods surgeon served as best he could for a small fee.

Along the Fox River Valley, where saws were ripping through logs from dawn to dusk in 31 mills, injuries were frequent. Medical men toiled for long hours daily trying to save lives.

This same condition was true in all other places that year, when 620 million feet of timber was being cut and sawed along the rivers called Wolf, Wisconsin, Menominee, Black, Mississippi, Chippewa, St. Croix, and Yellow.

For a young doctor without much practical experience as a surgeon in Green County, there were cruel challenges, with 21 sawmills heralding the advent of permanent industry for 23,000 inhabitants, who already had 16 flour mills, 4 woolen factories, 24 post offices, 123 schoolhouses, and 36 churches, with new settlers paying from $5 to $10 an acre for land.

At La Crosse, where 130 million feet of logs had been sealed in one single season, major surgery was a severe test for even a doctor who had been in the State Medical Society for many years.

Also, in the country of Waupaca, with 18 sawmills turning out 10 million feet of lumber yearly, many men were unable to avoid injury and surgical torture in spite of their safety consciousness.

Life was rough for a doctor at Peshtigo when treating frantic refugees for shock, injuries, and burns in what truly was a seething hell roaring through several counties in 1871, year of the Chicago fire.

Four years later, at Oshkosh, when flames nearly destroyed all the property in town, tireless medical men risked their own lives while rendering emergency service for persons injured or burned.

This was at a time when logging camps and sawmills were hooked up in an industry gigantic in scope, with the state's pine cut roughly estimated at 20 billion-board feet up to 1873, the number of mill workers to be increased from 7,748 to 40,000 during the peak years ahead, the number of mills to far exceed the 1873 total of 704, the yearly value of lumber to soar from $18,500,000 to $58,000,000.

Unfortunately, medical science wasn't moving along in a way that would insure meeting these challenges successfully. Major injuries were increasing greatly, with safety training unheard of and medical colleges still unable to offer much in both surgery and medicine. A humble company doctor was in a state of frustration while experimenting on a lumberjack's fractured spine or otherwise doing his duty in trying to relieve pain in a fractured neck bone or threatening to kill his patient by sawing off a gangrenous leg.

Yet some of Wisconsin's pioneer surgeons were truly great, showing exceptional skill under the severest of circumstances, and one of them was Nicholas Senn, who was in the town of Elmore when plank roads were being built.

In 1879, when heading the State Medical Society, Senn was a Milwaukeean, served by a pompous mail carrier, who wore a long sack coat of cadet gray. He had been a passenger in one of Milwaukee's earliest street cars driven by four horses over bumpy wooden rails.

Following in Dr. Senn's wake in Wisconsin during the latter part of the century were many outstanding surgeons. One was John Morris Dodd, a Pennsylvania farm boy, who, at 23, was graduated from Starling College in Columbus, Ohio. The time was 1889, just nine years after electric lights had been tried for the first time on Broadway in New York City.

Dodd's yearly tuition had been $50. Like others in his class, he had been admitted on a common-school diploma. His training was as good as that offered at any of the standard colleges of that day. His studies included obstetrics, gynecology, materia medica, chemistry, therapeutics, toxicology, pathology, physiology, anatomy, and hygiene.

Of the 14 members of that faculty at Starling, ten of them wore long, dangling, full beards, denoting dignity and distinction. Townsfolk knew them best by their Prince Albert coats and high silk hats.

Classrooms there were dingy. Lectures were given in musty rooms. High walls and ceilings were covered with dust, soot, and cobwebs. Clinics were musty. A carbolic spray was being used. Instruments were soaked in trays of carbolic-acid solution, one to 20. Hands were scrubbed in bichloride of mercury solution, one to 1,000. The professor of surgery wore no gloves, no cap, no mask. He did wear an apron.

At the time of his departure for North Wisconsin, young Dodd said, he was aware that people at large were rating their family doctors on a basis of their personalities, not on their remedies and their services.

Drugs were nauseous-fluid extracts and tart-tasting tinctures. Patients of that day were really punished by their doctors for being sick. They were living in a period known as therapeutic nihilism.

"One practicing physician carried in his little satchel two prescriptions for a single illness," Dodd said. "These two pills represented 20 different remedies, and both prescriptions were given to a patient at the same time."

As a doctor of *The Old School*, beginning his practice in Wisconsin, young John Dodd had become acquainted with antisepsis. He said he had much to learn concerning diseases—their causes, prevention, and cure.

Surgeons in Upper Wisconsin then dreaded to think of abdominal operations. Some of them even trembled when starting to cut through a patient's stomach wall.

In 1889, serum therapy was unknown, as were intravenous medications. A patient's blood pressure was estimated by the physician's touch. A full diagnosis consisted of: a look at the tongue, a feel of the pulse, taking the patient's temperature.

Appendicitis then was called perityphlitis. In 1890, doctors of North Wisconsin had learned a little about the tubercle bacillus, Dodd asserted in his autobiography, published in 1928 by Walter Neale of New York.

"*Homeopathy and eclecticism were at the height of their glory,*" he said. "*The bitterest competition was waged by devotees of the different schools. Today it is amusing to think how a doctor of one school would refuse to counsel with a doctor of another.*"

Regarding the physician's medicine case, Dodd declared:

"*It has become smaller with the doctor's years of practice; and the number of his remedies become less as he depends on certain drugs to produce certain effects. The old 'shotgun prescription' has given way to specific medication.*"

Going into Rhinelander, his starting place as a graduate of Starling College, at the age of 23, in need of wide knowledge concerning the germ theory of disease and proper methods for use in keeping bacteria out of wounds, Dr. Dodd started a little hospital of his own, with 12 beds in what actually was a good boarding house.

Men of the woods near-by paid him $5 to $10 a year for complete medical and hospital service, with a limit of six consecutive months of hospitalization at any one time, according to the insurance plan which was popular in the lumberjack country.

Dodd was both doctor and nurse, and the medical history of that region shows that his determination to keep his hospital sanitary was a trait which gained wide popularity for him.

Sawyers and axe wielders then were in the vicinity, making stately pine trees crash to ground.

After 18 months of practice there, young Dodd accepted an invitation from Dr. W. T. Rinehart to serve with him in a hospital of 75 beds in the boom sawmill city of Ashland, where Gov. Sam S. Fifield, Col. John H. Knight, and Dr. Edwin Ellis were making themselves immortal with their puissant leadership, successes, and prestige.

A graduate nurse was hired. A training school for nurses was set up.

Rinehart, preceptor at Starling College at the time of Dodd's enrollment, was now acquiring much knowledge concerning antiseptic surgery and improved operating-room techniques from Nicholas Senn, Wisconsin's most highly-skilled surgeon. For some time Rinehart had been in close touch with Dr. C. W. Oviatt of Oshkosh, whose reputation for skill, analysis, and reliability had been well advertised in that part of the state.

Rinehart and Dodd performed their first laparotomy while working together in an isolated farm house one night. This emergency operation was done in a kitchen. The patient was an old lady.

For authentic information concerning conditions of surgery as the gay nineties were going into the annals of history, let's read what scholarly Dr. Dodd has to say about it in the following paragraphs taken from his definitely interesting autobiography:

> Abdominal surgery rarely was attempted; but surgeons were steadily becoming bolder, and as hospital service improved, they did more of it.
>
> In the 80s and 90s, surgery was mostly emergency work. Hazardous occupations of sawmill and logging camp gave the doctors a large experience in the line of fractures, sprains, and wounds.
>
> Stomach surgery was in the development stage. The gall bladder was seldom invaded. Gallstones were treated with remedies. The appendix was becoming the subject of much study and experimental operation. Brain surgery was confined to raising the fragments of a depressed skull and to occasional trepanning.
>
> Amputations were common, because of the operators' lack of advanced knowl-

edge of asepsis and antisepsis in the treatment of fractures, etc.

Books on bacteriology were making their appearance; and one which I obtained early and studied extensively was by Dr. George M. Sternberg, surgeon-general of the army.

Medical literature was teeming with technique. Pelvic surgery was coming into vogue; and injuries due to childbirth were being cured by plastic surgery. Neoplasms of the uterus and ovaries were subjected to operation when found.

Ectopic pregnancy, with its ruptures, were treated on the expectant plan; and many a hematoma or resultant abscess were being evacuated by the vaginal route before we learned to go in and take up the ruptured tube, stop the hemorrhage, and remove the clots.

Later we learned that we could remove the fluid blood from the peritoneal sac, strain it of clots, and transfuse it into the patient's own veins, thus obviating in considerable degree the consequences of hemorrhage.

Science was moving swiftly, and we doctors were eagerly pursuing it, concluded Dr. Dodd.

In 1892 the Ashland Medical Society was founded, with Dodd as secretary, working closely with the state society, state board of health, and the American Medical Association.

A typhoid-fever epidemic, striking Ashlanders in a devastating manner in 1893, nearly killed Dr. Dodd, who, like other self-sacrificing men in that profession, were taking great risks, so their patients could successfully resist the challenges of death.

Trained nurses were scarce. Training schools were being set up in the larger hospitals of the state.

In managing to keep his mortality rate down to zero in his first 100 cases of typhoid fever, Dr. Dodd had his patients on a program of confinement to bed, milk diet, intestinal antisepsis, and careful nursing; he kept the temperature under control by bathing.

Indeed this was a wonderful achievement in the advent of country-wide vaccination and a more rigid program of sanitation. Highly efficient nursing also had proved its importance in a fight against plague, which at Ashland was recurring each fall.

This epidemic of typhoid fever began in unsanitary lumber camps, where flies were germ carriers, working out of kitchens, dump piles, and outhouses.

Dr. Dodd's story concerning the appalling Ashland situation brings to light the following cruel 1892 epidemic facts, as told by him:

> Without proper disinfection, the discharges of typhoid-fever patients were thrown into the sewer and carried into the bay, which was the source of Ashland's water supply.
>
> Within two or three weeks from the time patients from logging camps commenced to arrive at the hospitals, typhoid began to make its appearance throughout the city.
>
> True, the intake pipe extended a mile out into the bay, where the water was supposed to be taken in; but this pipe was laid on the bottom of the bay, and dragging anchors of ships occasionally would break it apart. Then polluted water from the near shore was admitted into the pipe.
>
> Finally the intake-water pipe was buried six feet deep, in a trench dredged in the bottom of the lake, which secured it from injury. A filtration plant, with chlorinization of the water, was added. Then the typhoid-fever epidemics disappeared.

DR. JOHN MORRIS DODD

whose fight for medical progress virtually was the foundation for his immortality.

At his hospital, Dr. Dodd had a program of careful disinfection of all infectious discharges; he repeatedly made known to the public that the most active agent in the dissemination of typhoid was the housefly.

"The presence of a housefly on the dining table or in the kitchen is the signal for hostilities until the fly has been killed," the Ashland doctor said.

His bacteriology research extensive and his initiative steadfastly strong as he advocated safe health measures, Dr. Dodd was greatly disturbed when seeing an Ashland grocer display fruit in bushel baskets in front of his store, allowing the street air and blowing dust to deposit germs on his apples, peaches, cherries, plums, and pears from early morning until dusk.

One day, after telling this grocer that the greatest of all destroyers—disease germs—are in the air, and that a health hazard is created for customers when buying fruit taken from a basket in the street, the doctor was rebuked.

It was another instance in which one person, without adequate knowledge, perception, and proper attitude, was unwilling to accept some sound advice from an expert and friend who was trying to do some good.

Added to the irony was the fact that each day on this particular city street sickly men were spitting on sidewalks and street. Tuberculosis was quite prevalent there.

Those were the days when an Ashland health officer was having painted on walks along the main street an admonition as follows: "Don't spit on the walks!"

Men, puffing on big cigars while in conversation with others in front of fruit-stand display, had been known to spit into the street regularly between comments; and as one medical commentator remarked: "A man I know is doing his best to give his TB germs to as many others as he can."

Early in this century, when clinics were set up in various Wisconsin cities, Dr. Dodd established the first one at Ashland; and when the University of Wisconsin was in its pioneer medical-training stage, Dodd and others around the state gave student doctors an opportunity to get the benefit of their surgical techniques. The different clinics, in fact, did much to help the state university to finally reach the medical-training standards which long had been awaited. The first ones were located at Ashland, Eau Claire, Wausau, Marshfield, La Crosse, Milwaukee, Sheboygan, and Statesan.

Most doctors then, as now, ate at irregular hours; they were deprived of the proper amounts of sleep, had little or no time for music, made maximum sacrifices, so that sick people could get well. Moreover, most of them were not of great wealth.

Fighting quackery in the first decade of the twentieth century required as much time as research in both medicine and surgery; and all of these duties had to be accomplished between calls at the office and at the hospitals.

Probably the most aggravating of quack phases everywhere was that of the so-called medicine show, offered by fakers who traveled from place to place, displaying dead tapeworms in bottles containing a chemical solution, shouting to their listeners from a platform an endless amount of statements concerning the presence of a tapeworm in everyone's body.

Warnings were to the effect that, if the persons listening did not get rid of their tapeworms immediately, they would be shortening their earthly lives by many years.

Actually, the quacks told them, no doctor could cure whatever ailments they had later, because of the destruction which tapeworms were certain to cause.

Therefore, as a needed safety measure, eliminating the biggest hazard at the basic source, it was the duty of every person present to buy a medicine that would kill tapeworms and thus prevent the kind of body damage which, said the fakers, would result in early death, regardless of how capable were the doctors.

The wonder medicine sold for $1 a bottle.

At Ashland, night after night, from Monday through Saturday, hundreds of men and women came to the platform near the Bardon Hose House to make a purchase. They went home with a bottle containing a fluid preparation comparable to the effectiveness of saltpeter. Profits for two showmen and one woman were enormous, since their platform costs were comparatively nothing—a small amount being paid for the rental of a vacant lot long neglected, as proven by its weeds.

All in all it was a sight cruel to behold, said the disgusted medical men of that town; and the most disturbed physician there probably was Dr. Dodd, who was at the show place at reasonable intervals, studying the full extent of the buffoonery and the gullibility of adults who, in daily life, had been known to be sensible.

Dodd brought this matter to the attention of brother members in the State Medical Society, urging a state-wide war on this new type of ugly sin.

Like other country doctors of that day, he had been riding a Springfield bicycle, called a roadster, a substitute for the horse and buggy, with a large wheel in front and a small one behind. To be thrown from it—over the handlebars, with one's kit, was an experience of no small embarrassment and hurt.

Dodd, with limitless energy, went onward to the presidency of the State Medical Society in 1912. The next year he was on the Wisconsin State Board of Medical Examiners. As mayor of Ashland, he built a park system which became noted for its beauty. He kept stressing the importance of sanitation, adequate ventilation of buildings, the isolation of patients suffering from infectious diseases, strong health controls. As physician-surgeon for the Soo Railroad Company, he made a trip to London to participate in an international clinic. For decades he was on the Northland College Board of Trustees. Most noteworthy were his puissant virtues of dignity and poise when confronted with disturbing factors.

No one ever saw Dr. Dodd in a sullen mood. Tragic events didn't dull his outlook in any way, didn't damage his heart. He saw vast forests destroyed by fire. He fought smallpox valiantly for the public when that epidemic was causing big logging camps to close. In an operating room during a dark surgical era, Dodd saw injured men in agony, unable to stay alive, because of the inefficiency of science, with no indication as to when science would eliminate the torture caused by a surgeon's crude tools.

As a general practitioner in days when a specialist was unknown, Dr. Dodd did everything but eye work. For many years he had no X-rays to help him in determining the extent of fractures. Until 1895, when Wilhelm K. Roentgen, University of Wurzburg professor, made known his creative greatness, X-rays were unknown.

Anyone in the pre-Roentgen era who may have had any doubts about the future of medicine in Wisconsin should have seen Dr. Harmon Van Dusen in action. His central point of activity was historic Mineral Point.

In his third successive term as State Medical Society head, in 1869, Van Dusen was spearheading a movement to protect the public from indiscriminate sale of poisons. A powerful crusader, he had the courage to face strong opposition. The following resolution, recommended by him and quickly passed by State Medical Society members, was sent to the legislature:

"That a measure be enacted to prohibit the traffic in obscene literature, disgusting advertisements, and other articles of indecent and immoral use, as well as obscene advertisements of patent medicine."

The state society's gospel of cleanliness was spreading. Dissections were legalized. Action was initiated to set up a State Board of Examiners.

Diphtheria, coming back to imperil the Wisconsin public, took the lives of 2,202 persons in 1881. This crisis was in the wake of that panic which began to stagger the nation financially in 1872.

Doctors in time were mentioning the discovery in the blood of a germ that causes relapsing fever. Later the bacillus of leprosy was discovered. Most vital for people of Wisconsin was a newspaper story concerning discovery of the bacillus of typhoid fever.

Discovery of the pneumonia germ soon was followed by an announcement relating to the bacillus of tuberculosis. Doctors everywhere were acquiring knowledge concerning successful treatment for epidemics which once were on the rampage. Finally a steam atomizer was in use for the spraying of carbolic acid.

At the University of Wisconsin, a course in natural history was being conducted by Edward A. Birge, who had been working in Agassiz's Harvard University laboratory. This achievement in faculty staffing was being credited to President Bascom. He gave Dr. Birge a professorship in zoology. Birge's background of study included personal findings at Leipzig, Germany.

As for state-wide medical progress in the ensuing years, it is best reflected in action taken by State Medical Society leaders, whose great achievements included efforts to set up an effective tuberculosis control, public education in combating tuberculosis, legislation to establish a state board of examiners exclusively in the field of tuberculosis, care of alcoholics, a hospital for inebriates, a postgraduate medical instruction program for the University of Wisconsin, a study of compulsory-health insurance, a movement to set up the highest standards for internship, legislation for the hospital care of indigent sick, suitable provision for the care and treatment of epileptic cases, a bill to establish a state medical-grievance committee, extensive surveys of welfare and health conditions throughout state, continuously broad studies, and planned corrective action.

Wisconsin physicians actually were responsible for the creation by the American Medical Association of a council on physical therapy. Another marked achievement was in the law enacted by the legislature in 1925 concerning the basic knowledge required of all Wisconsin doctors in treating the sick. This basic law was the first of its kind in our nation.

Playing a prominent roll during this magnetic period of transition was Dr. William E. Ground of Superior, who in 1908 was elevated to the leadership of the State Medical Society.

What a giant in the fields of training, experience, and success! What a public servant!

In the winter of 1887 and 1888, with six years of practice behind him, Dr. Ground was at King's College in London, studying the methods of surgery being used there by Dr. Lister. He saw Lister in action and heard him explain the proper use of his carbolic spray. Ground saw Lister scrub and rinse his hands in diluted carbolic acid before an operation. Lister wore no gloves, no face mask, no cap, no black frock.

"In the late 1880s and early 90s," Dr. Ground told historians, "surgeons in this country had bare hands when operating. Those with long whiskers, implying that stubble on the face was evidence of virility and inspiring manhood, were following old rock-ribbed traditions. They created hazards for their patients by allowing whiskers to dangle in the incisions."

In that era, which marked the assassination of President Garfield, surgeons were using aromatic spirits of ammonia and whiskey in operating rooms.

Interesting is this account of crude surgery in President Garfield's case, written by Dr. William E. Ground during the State Medical Society's centennial observance:

> Within five minutes after the shooting, the president was given aromatic spirits of ammonia and whiskey. The bullet, entering his back between the tenth and eleventh ribs, was embedded under the splenic artery. The surgeons, while trying to find it, were handicapped by a lack of knowledge.
>
> Antiseptic rules were not clearly defined. During the process of probing, the president developed fever and chills. A tract was discovered leading down the back. It was the route of the deflected ball; but the ball was not found. Each day this cavity was irrigated and washed out. A veritable pus sac was formed. Finally the patient, after suffering for eleven weeks, died of exhaustion. Not until an autopsy was conducted was the bullet found.
>
> If the attending surgeons had had a clear conception of antiseptic surgery, they would have known that, after the bullet had gone through to the tissue and stopped, it had done its worst; and when the surgeons were meddling with the wound in a crude manner, they actually were provoking and speeding infection.

The man who wrote this was a surgeon of great rank. For many decades the city of Superior gained prestige through his practice, his philosophy, his kindness, his influence, his warmth. To him goes a lasting bugler's salute. Another bulwark of influence was Arthur Helm of Beloit. So were W. P. Sperry, Phillips; H. G. Mertens and Henry Hannum, Bayfield; A. A. Dye and Philip Fox, Madison; Erastus B. Wolcott, kidney specialist, who in 1861 became world renowned when performing the first nephrectomy in a Milwaukee hospital; William Snow Miller, University of Wisconsin professor of anatomy, known throughout our nation for his systematization of lung physiology, whose priceless collection of medical books has become a part of the state university's library of medicine.

The honor list is long. It includes Francis Fischer, Madisonian, who, at the time of his death in 1879, had lived during that era when adulteration generally was rampant, with nearly all common foodstuffs adulterated.

Doctor Fischer did not live to see Edison's electric light; and when sick persons were getting word to him concerning medical needs, they had to do so by way of a horse and buggy, or by foot, for telephones were unknown.

In the crusades of that day, Francis Fischer was giving his full support. So was John Favill, a graduate of Howard Medical College, a Madisonian, who headed the State Medical Society in 1872 and was followed by M. Waterhouse, Portage; J. T. Reeve, Appleton; and J. B. Whiting, Janesville, in that order.

Rush Medical College then was best known for its excellency of faculty and student body. Foremost as a professor was Christian Fenger, a bacteriologist, expert in the use of microscope, whose skill in performing an autopsy was unsurpassed. One of his students was Nicholas Senn. Another was J. B. Murphy, pride of Appleton, christened in a small log church, who, when taking his college-entrance examination, was with youngsters who wore side whiskers.

Murphy's internship in the pre-asepsis era was at Cook County Hospital, Chicago, where puerperal infections were known to be frightfully frequent and deadly. In years that followed, when arguments concerning appendicitis were dividing the doctors into two groups, one of which recommended an operation, the other voicing strong objection,

"J. B." contended that early operative treatment was the way to save lives. A steadfast defender of his faith, he caused his opponents to nickname him "Stormy Petrel."

As a humble physician to the poor, Dr. Murphy lived to know the reward of his many struggles. Wisconsin's village doctors, too, warmed their hearts by saving lives. While traveling a great distance on a train, they all were thankful for the service rendered, with a wood burner pulling the cars and stopping every 15 miles for cordwood and water.

Railroad transportation then was a huge improvement over the old stagecoach travel; and when streets at La Crosse were paved with kerosene-soaked shavings and sawdust, people there were grateful for the paving improvements which city officials had brought about for them.

With reference again to the great contributions made by Wisconsin doctors outside of their profession in those decades of the 19th century, the record of J. B. Bowen in business and government at Madison is one of high merit. In 1871 he was mayor; and at the time of his death in '81, he left an influence which was long remembered by all those who knew him.

Medicine dispensed in Dr. Bowen's day was bitter-tasting tincture. Pains in the appendix and in other vital parts of the abdomen were called stomach trouble. Surgeons didn't operate on these parts; and peritonites was a death sentence. In approximately 43% of the nation's cases, an amputation quickly meant a casket, a mortician's service, and grave.

The story of penicillin couldn't be told during Dr. Bowen's lifetime. The discovery of this wonder drug by Alexander Fleming, English bacteriologist, was not to become a reality until a half century after the death of Dr. Bowen.

The fight against disease was of the toughest; and just as the life of a patient was in the doctor's hands, every community relied on its medical men to keep its people strong.

The town of Elmore in Fond du Lac county was fortunate in having as its leader a man of rare medical ability and skill, who in 1879 was president of the State Medical Society. Later he gained national prominence as a physician in private practice in Milwaukee and Chicago. He was

Nicholas Senn. During his military service, he was the Army's best-rated surgeon.

Achievements credited to Senn by societies outside of Wisconsin, more particularly the Texas Medical Association, include closure of intestinal perforations, in typhoid fever; intravenous and intra-arterial injection for intestinal obstruction.

Senn's personal history was that of an immortal; and after his departure from the Wisconsin scene, medical giants kept coming on here. They included Stephen E. Gavin of Fond du Lac, Kate Pelham Newcomb of the Mercer-Woodruff-Minocqua area, Raymond G. Arveson of Frederic, and James Jackson of Madison.

Arveson's status was well portrayed by Dr. A. H. Heidner of West Bend, who, in presenting a Council Award to the humble Frederic doctor before the State Medical Society's House of Delegates on May 9, 1957, asserted:

> This Council Award is the highest honor which the State Medical Society of Wisconsin can bestow upon one of its members. It is granted only upon occasion. It is for those who, in an exemplary way, have served their fellow physicians, medical science, and the public.
>
> In the 28 years since the Council Award was established, 24 awards have been made. It may be said of those who have been its recipients that they have personified the highest traditions of medicine in their devotion to the public good.
>
> Tonight, by direction of my fellow councilors, we give another Council Award. We present it to Raymond Gregory Arveson, a son of Minnesota, whose grandfather and great-grandfather before him were doctors of medicine.
>
> Distinguished in his attainments as a physician and a surgeon, Dr. Arveson is

a graduate of the Wisconsin College of Physicians and Surgeons, which later became Marquette School of Medicine.

He is a Navy veteran of World War I, the first Wisconsin physician to build a small hospital in which to start a rural-group practice, the great chairman of the Society's first Special Committee to Study the Distribution of Health Service and Sickness Care.

This Committee headed by Dr. Arveson has searched Wisconsin and the nation to discover improved scientific and economic means of bringing better health care to the people of this state.

A member of the State Board of Medical Examiners from 1941 to 1948, president of the State Medical Society in 1940, a Society councilor since 1942, president of the Village of Frederic for 18 years, a member of the Frederic school board and numerous other civic positions, Dr. Arveson was a member of the Board of Regents of the University of Wisconsin for eight and one-half years.

He has been an outstanding leader in the affairs of the Polk County Medical Society, the State Medical Society of Wisconsin, the American Medical Association, the American College of Surgeons, and the Interstate Postgraduate Medical Association of North America.

The physician who is Doctor Arveson is described best, perhaps, in an address by J. George Crownhart, first full-time secretary of the State Medical Society of Wisconsin. This address was given at a community gathering in Frederic to honor the conclusion of Dr. Arveson's term as president of our Society. Said Crown-

FREDERIC'S DR. R. G. ARVESON

whose philosophy of life and of medicine is in reality a guide for the advancement of the welfare of our people.

hart: "Because this man had tolerance did not mean to him that he must suppress the courage of his convictions; and so, within medicine, as within your own community, Arveson fought for his ideals. He pointed out time and time again, until the truth of his statement was fully appreciated, that medicine must be more than a hospital. He emphasized that, as valuable as is the aid, the laboratory is not medicine. He revivified to the profession of Wisconsin that the family physician reached the heights of the ideals of medicine when recognizing the limitations of any one man in a science so broad. Yes, Dr. Arveson centered upon the sound care, the bedside attention, and the human understanding of men, women and little children, so that he was enabled to successfully treat the 90 per cent of ills to which we all fall common heir, leaving to others the occasional case that requires the specialist."

At this point in his ceremony, Dr. Heidner talked directly to awardee Arveson, saying: For your unfailing loyalty and devotion to the practice of medicine, for your extraordinary zeal and leadership in bringing to the people better medical care at a price they can afford to pay, for your high honesty and innate fairness, for the inspiration and vision you have given to home, church, community, profession and state, we, your fellow members, give you this seal of our Society as a token of your achievement and of our esteem and affection.

In this tribute, the people of Wisconsin are deeply appreciative. They salute Frederic's beloved public servant, whose long span of life has been distinguished by community leadership in government, culture, and education while easing pain, prolonging life, putting warmth into the hearts of the sick, strengthening his own virtues of unselfishness, faith, courage, humility, poise, resources, and appropriate tolerance levels.

Surely human history has had an important chapter added to it by Frederic's dedicated country doctor, whose practice is in a region of enchanting lakes, rushing streams, and rich agricultural fertility—once a key area for the North West Company of fur traders, where prolonged suffering, hunger, uncertainty, fear, well-organized sin, ruthlessness, and tragedy marked the most desperate stage of competition between Bourgeois Sayer of the North West Company and Commi Curot of the X Y.

Since those dismal wilderness days, with the panorama of Wisconsin history extending over a century and a half, progress has been unlimited, currently standing out like a colossus. It is well illustrated in the philosophy of Dr. Arveson and others of that school of thought who, in the past, have made our State Medical Society a puissant force in the development of our state.

Strong men of medicine, with miracle drugs and vastly-improved surgical techniques, have given us an opportunity to live in a golden age.

Helping to make this a golden age was kind, courageous, enduring Dr. Kate Pelham Newcomb, staunch friend of the poor. On numerous occasions each winter, she risked injury and death during an emergency in sub-zero weather by traveling on snowshoes over snow-packed, gravel roads through a blinding blizzard for many miles at night in the lonely backwoods area of Boulder Junction, Winegar, Mercer, Manitowish, Woodruff, and Minocqua during the economical collapse of the 1930s and the fretful World War years of the 1940s.

When duty called, Dr. Kate was on the road. No storm and no other adverse condition in the darkness of a forest night could prevent her from doing what she felt was her responsibility in the eyes of God in what the confident and thankful inhabitants called God's country.

A case of pneumonia in a hard-to-reach farm house 20 miles away had to be treated as soon as Kate's automobile and snowshoes could take her there. Delivery of a baby had to be accomplished in accordance with the established medical standards, no matter how high the banks of snow, how low the temperature, how severe the fatigue.

One of the most benevolent doctors the world has ever known, with inexhaustible courage and endurance, viewing self sacrifice and kindness in the manner of Hippocrates, *The Father of Medicine*, Dr. Kate was the only practitioner in that region. In time she set up a regular circuit, driving as many as 100 miles a day, going over unplowed side roads in winter after a storm, shoveling a path into an isolated farmhouse, treating sick Indians who gave blankets, moccasins, and beads as their pay, setting lumberjacks' broken bones, easing the pain of homesteaders and farmers who were feebly combating the ravages of the depression. Often these white people of the woods gave cordwood, chickens, eggs, and vegetables in return for medical services rendered.

With her span of activities ever broadening, Dr. Kate Pelham Newcomb set up an office in each of six village halls and in schoolhouses. On those scheduled days when she was on duty there, patients converged from many far-inland points.

The closest hospitals were at Rhinelander and Tomahawk, 30 to 60 miles away, where Dr. Kate performed most of her operations. In several instances of emergency, she delivered a baby in her car. During her backwoods Wisconsin career, more than 3,000 babies were delivered. Not a single mother was lost.

Boosters at Woodruff finally began to stress the need for a hospital there, and to get a project under way, a Chicago industrialist in 1949 donated $100. Then the Lions Club sponsored a drive for gifts. Hustlers in outlying places held dances and other benefit events. Within a short time, the fund totaled nearly $5,000. It was enough to warrant breaking ground on the construction site; and when the actual work was begun, volunteers appeared with timber, cinder blocks, and mortar, which they themselves had donated.

Snowstorms caused the building operations to cease. A regular topic at the Woodruff high school in the days that followed concerned a campaign for additional funds. A girl suggested a drive for a million pennies. This idea was adopted by the student body. Money acquired through woodcutting, delivery service, chores, and baby sitting eventually was an amazingly large sum. The nation's greatest penny parade kept rolling along. When it ended, 1,200,000 copper pennies, four and a half tons of them, were dumped on the high-school, gymnasium floor.

Donations were pouring in from all parts of Wisconsin, causing the villagers of Minocqua, Woodruff, Boulder Junction, Arbor Vitae, and Mercer to celebrate in a pompous way. More than 20,000 hustlers saw a gala parade. Then they spearheaded a drive for additional funds. Hospital-construction work was resumed. Plans were enlarged. They called for an increased number of beds and adequate operating-room equipment, with oxygen piped into every room.

High public officials, seeking nation-wide attention in an effort to acquire a deluge of donations, contacted Ralph Edwards, conductor of *This Is Your Life* in Hollywood. In due time, as the result of a perfect hoax, Dr. Kate was lured into a surprise appearance on NBC's Television Show. Edwards introduced her on 20 million TV screens. He told the story of her life. He explained the idea behind the Woodruff-Arbor Vitae students' million-penny parade. There was a suggestion that people of all America donate as many pennies as they could. The resultant response generally was symbolic of NBC prestige. From every state in the union and from 23 foreign countries came currency, piggy-bank savings, and pennies that were taped to cardboard.

In a pine-tree environment at Woodruff later, Dr. Kate was greeted by a flabbergasted throng which represented every community in that vast land of lakes. She was escorted to the Woodruff-Arbor Vitae, high school gymnasium, where 200 volunteers were standing on a big mound of coins, sorting the different pieces into their respective bins, voicing ecstacy as the nation's most spectacular accounting feature was under way, lauding Ralph Edwards, and staying on the job until coins valued at tens of thousands of dollars had been counted.

Dr. Kate, with eyes tear-laden and emotions hard to conceal, said she was overawed. She couldn't stay long. A man in the backwoods, 26 miles away, had just phoned, saying his pregnant wife was in severe pain. So off rushed Kate, with her medicine kit and supplies.

Days later she was dead. She had broken a hip in a fall on sidewalk ice. For her, life had ended on an operating table. Her assistant, Mercer's Dr. Wm. G. Hiatt, carried out the plans which 1,200,000 copper pennies had brought to completion.

Adele Comandini's book, *Dr. Kate—An Angel on Snowshoes*, is something all should read.

Doctor Kate, while serving the sick in an unprecedented way, had walked humbly with God. Her name forever will be emblazoned on the honor rolls of the art of healing.

In retrospect now our medical profession's historical data looms like the pyramid of Gizeh in size.

Entrance of Cornelius A. Harper as a student in the University of Wisconsin Medical School in 1885 was of broad significance, for he was a youngster whose scholarship and trusted leadership eventually was to take him into the state service as Health Officer of exceptionally long tenure.

As a 21-year-old farmer and schoolteacher from Hazel Green, Harper was the son of a university-educated father, who had migrated from Pennsylvania to Wisconsin with his family by way of the Ohio and Mississippi rivers in that year when Wisconsin passed from territorial to state government.

Formal study for Cornelius as a grade-school boy at Hazel Green was intermittent. A student there usually enrolled late in December. His classroom work was completed on the first day of March, so as to permit him to work on a farm.

Rain, hail, and snowstorms, too, made school attendance irregular at country schools, thus reducing the extent of benefits to be derived in a course of two full months.

When going aboard a train bound for Madison in '85 for the purpose of writing an entrance test, young Harper was experiencing his first long trip away from home. Previously he had not traveled more than 12 miles. As a schoolteacher near Cuba City, his monthly salary was $40.

By the time he had completed his medical studies at Wisconsin, with a B.S. degree, the entire medical course had been overhauled. Special sciences were added. Surgery was best known for its vast number of needed discoveries.

When assuming state office, following additional study and training at the Columbian Medical School in Washington, D. C., Dr. Harper had a job of huge proportions. People at large had to be informed regularly concerning health hazards, elimination of false ideas, personal needs, opportunities for health improvement. Old fallacies had to be fought through an educational service. The average death rate had to be reduced considerably.

In time of epidemic, when city health officials everywhere needed the best possible informational service from the state as an aid in setting up controls, Dr. Harper's understaffed department was expected to excel in medical leadership.

At the turn of this century, in fact, the field of medicine was still in its pioneer stage, although far ahead of its pre-Lister era. Public-health needs, increasing with the population, required endless planning and intense work, broader medical knowledge, better objectives in the prevention and cure of disease, so as to prolong life, ease pain, give comfort to the sick.

Oddly enough, the State Board of Health was not easy to create. In spite of the prestige which its sponsor, the State Medical Society, had built up through great achievements, certain political leaders in the legislature did their best to block passage of the bill which specified the establishment of a state health department.

This condition is best shown in certain events leading up to final legislative action. The governor didn't like the Sauk county assemblyman who was in the forefront, urging passage. In making known his personal views, he was indicating opposition to the bill; and when Dr. Teal of Sauk County came into the legislature to develop favorable interest, the governor accused him of seeking political gain. Harsh feelings developed.

The governor, with a wrong interpretation of events, regarded Dr. Teal as a nuisance. Yet the undaunted country doctor kept working hard as a crusader, seeking the best possible public-health service for the people of his state. He himself was the one who originally had caused the Sauk

County assemblyman to introduce the bill. Not many physicians of that day, obviously, were willing to appear in public as fighters for a cause which involved the legislature.

This bill finally passed, it empowered a part-time medical director to appoint a stenographer, salaried at $40 per month; and a secretary, who was Dr. J. T. Reeve of Appleton, holder of the position for 18 years. A general yearly fund of $3,000 was set up for the board.

Opponents of this measure, surely, were not health students; and unfortunately for these poorly informed politicians, they did not know the true medical needs of their state. They were unable to vision the reasons why their state university was urgently in need of a medical course for young men wishing to be doctors.

Undoubtedly these same obstructionists did not know the seriousness of the country's medical situation many years before when a Boston physician told his fellow practitioners the following:

"Our process of education is far behind the times.

"I sincerely believe that the unbiased opinion of most medical men of sound judgment and long experience is that the amount of death and disaster in this world now would be less if all diseases were left alone. Our medical profession is under the multiform, reckless and contradictory modes of practice, good and bad, with which practitioners of adverse denominations carry on their differences at the expense of the patients."

Incidentally, how would you like to have been living in that experimental era, often referred to by oldtimers as "good old"?

Attacking public adversity was a rough, humiliating activity for medical leaders of that era. Negative-minded legislators had to be fought along with disease, epidemics, quackery, and false traditions. One big struggle continuously was against devastating epidemics.

In 1901, when Dr. J. F. Pritchard of Manitowoc was president of the State Medical Society, following the term of W. T. Sarles of Sparta, diphtheria and typhoid fever were still uncontrolled; and at regular intervals an epidemic was striking some part of the state with alarming results. Each new epidemic was more severe than the last one, killing a greater number of victims and spreading over a wider area of homes.

That was the biggest challenge confronting Dr. Cornelius Harper when appointed secretary of the State Board of Health. For many years, prior to the marketing of miracle drugs and the establishment of definite controls, these complex problems were not being met successfully. In 1910, it seemed, diphtheria and typhoid fever together would put approximately 20,000 Wisconsin citizens in their graves during the next 30 years unless brought under control.

From a standpoint of general health conditions, the year 1910 was seriously adverse in many ways. For example, a report published by the American Medical Association disclosed that 155 institutions of learning in the United States and Canada had been granting medical degrees on a basis of superficial training and inadequate equipment. A betrayal of public trust had been noteworthy in those colleges. A wide range of hazards had been created for the medical profession at large.

Tartly enough, all of these colleges and universities, guilty of medical neglect and inefficiency, had exorbitant student fees.

As late as 1910, the American Medical Association had been waging a consistently strong fight against many unfavorable conditions afield, more particularly in the hospitals of this country. Long, overdue crusades were under way.

In fact, a half century had passed since the introduction of high hospital standards by Florence Nightingale, who, in 1854, as a 34-year-old nurse with the British army during the Crimean war, inspected wards for food, housing, and health conditions, dedicated her work to the welfare of private soldiers, and later founded what is now known as modern nursing by starting a training school of her own.

In this country, Miss Nightingale's influence finally was being felt, especially when an epidemic was imperiling a town.

In 1910 the number of typhoid-fever cases in Wisconsin was 2,446. Deaths totaled 558. The mortality rate was high, with approximately one out of every four patients failing to survive.

Diphtheria cases, too, were shockingly large in number that year, and 429 patients died as the result of inadequate drugs and the destructiveness of diphtheria germs.

Five years later, in 1915, when Doctors Arthur J. Patek of Milwaukee and Charles S. Sheldon of Madison were aggressive leaders in the State Medical Society, problems were enormous. One was tuberculosis, which made necessary a long series of crusades throughout the state, led by the Wisconsin Anti-Tuberculosis Association.

Most prominent in this crusade was Dr. John M. Beffel of Milwaukee, a tireless speaker, whose theme "The Ravages of the Great White Plague" caused health workers in all counties to preach sanitation, safety, and sagacity.

Warring on uncleanliness in public eating places, Dr. Beffel stressed the dangers of tubercular germs. Servers of food and drink were told to properly sterilize their customers' drinking glasses and cups, dishes, forks, knives and spoons.

Of Pasteur's school of thought, lauding Dr. Lister for his accomplishments in the overall program of prolonging life and adding comfort to it, Crusader Beffel spent much time as a public speaker. He told about lung infections and how persons suffering from these diseases are infectious to others. Sufferers, he said, expel the causative organism into their surroundings by way of the cough and the sneeze; and when inhaled by other persons, the tubercle bacillus and the pneumococcus cause dangerous infection.

This information, widely circulated with many other facts by Beffel and his aids, had beneficial effects. It was released to the press in deftly written articles by Louise Fenton Brand, an administrative official, who formerly had been with the Milwaukee Sentinel as city editor.

In later years, Dr. Louis M. Warfield, a graduate of the Johns Hopkins University School of Medicine, became actively identified with the Wisconsin Anti-Tuberculosis Association; and in this capacity, he was a pioneer of prominence, a man of both quality and distinction.

In the crusade against tuberculosis, one great victory finally was scored in the pasteurization of milk. It was strengthened by rigid pure-food laws. Discovery of brucellosis in cows placed more emphasis on protected dairy products; and when a state law made necessary the testing of all cows for milk-borne diseases and the destruction of all animals found infected, bacteria in Wisconsin's dairy field was under well-organized controls.

In other fields, infection-spreading organisms were on a deadly march. They thrived on human weaknesses. Virtually they were more prevalent than man's sin.

One particular virus, that of influenza, suddenly turned lethal. During the winter of 1918-1919, when American soldiers were defying the horrors of both war and disease, flu struck 20 million citizens of this country. It killed 850,000.

Against this type of flu, there was immunity for nobody. There was no defense, no preventive drug, no vaccine. Pain couldn't be eased, and the battle against fever was best known by the fright which it created. It damaged the patient's heart.

Complications, chiefly pneumonia, caused most of the fatalities. For men of the armed forces, death via influenza was more horrible than death by way of an enemy's hand grenade or machine-gun bullets. Army doctors, in seeking to save lives, used as much whiskey as they could acquire. Throughout the world, 20 million flu sufferers succumbed. Their hearts were suddenly stopped by a virus so small that only the most powerful microscope could spot it.

So devastating was the germ that its victims frequently died a day or two after being disabled. Lung cavities quickly were flooded with blood. Tissues were ripped and scoured as if struck by poison gas. Pneumonia, in these cases, didn't have an opportunity to expand its casualty list.

Medical scientists, baffled by this situation, were then in the process of developing a defense called vaccine. Just as they had conquered smallpox, diphtheria, and typhoid fever, it was up to them now to wipe out influenza.

What a project! And what a mammoth goal generally —the prevention of chronic illness, easing pain, prolonging life!

Indeed, progress couldn't be retarded. Tonsillectomy, for example, had to be so improved that the patient regarded it as something to be accepted, not something frightful.

Are you old enough to remember some of the techniques which, in decades agone, were in need of revision?

When telling a doctor that some condition within you had caused you to become ill, were you asked to show your tongue?

Was your tongue coated?

Today, when seeking to determine your child's ailment, are you carefully examining that movable muscular organ on the floor of the mouth subserving the special sense of taste and aiding in mastication, deglutition, and the articulation of sound—that same muscular asset which is attached to the hyoid bone by muscles, to the epiglottis by the glossoepiglottic folds, to the soft palate by the anterior pillars? Do you have remedies of your own, concocting them in the kitchen?

If the answers are yes, shame on you!

Let your doctor see that coated tongue and, in his approved medical way, he will do what he knows is best. He will not rely on the tongue for a hint as to what particular medical treatment is needed. His diagnosis will be very broad, reaching the ailment at its basic source. He knows that inflamed tonsils, sinus, bronchitis, mouth ulcers, fever, flu, and other conditions can cause a coated tongue.

Determining an underlying cause is the responsibility of the family physician, not pa or ma. Safety in prescription is that given by a doctor, not a medically untrained parent.

In this mention of old, false traditions, together with the slow advances being made by medical science up to the discovery of wonder drugs, improved diagnosis, and amazing surgical accomplishments, it is easy to understand why life expectancy was not an inspiring topic.

Oldtimers, those who were hit hard by scarlet fever early in this century, can remember two serious complications — heart and kidneys — that had to be diligently watched. Today, such complications in scarlet fever cases are uncommon. Our drugs are that good. Caution, however, is wise. Excessive activity, doctors say, should be avoided during the convalescence period.

PART IV

MIRACLE DRUGS
MIRACLE SURGERY

In 1956, according to a report submitted by the American Medical Association, the number of deaths due to appendicitis in this country was 2,200. Most of them could have been prevented if early medical treatment had been sought.

For many years preventive medicine has been the heart of public health. It has been a sound investment; and the amazing progress made in anesthesia lately has been another factor in a prediction that medicine eventually will break the age barrier. In time, our public-health prophets say, people will reach the age of 150.

As an illustration of this trend, the temperature of a 64-year-old man in Brooklyn suddenly soared to 107 degrees overnight while awaiting surgery. Icepacks and other methods failed to bring it down. For use in this special case, the hospital engineer adapted a hypothermia machine, ordinarily used to chill patients booked for surgery. Within six hours, the man's temperature was normal again, hospital authorities said. The machine works like a refrigeration unit, with the patient wrapped in a rubberized mat in which a refrigerant is circulated through inner coils.

The patient was blessed real good. Now he seeks to make old age healthier and more satisfying. He demands as much life here on earth as he possibly can get, with the aid of a medical profession that has devoted itself superbly to the cause of good health, conquering pain, epidemics, germs, surgical problems, and disease.

People of Wisconsin are seeking to enhance the satisfaction and joy of life. They are saluting the University of Wisconsin Medical School, Marquette University, state and county medical societies, training schools for nurses, public-health officials, and the many thousands of doctors and nurses who, in past and present, have given their work lives to people who have been sick. Because of them, Wisconsin has ranked among the nation's best defenders of public health. The full history of medicine here has been encyclopedic in scope, with one extraordinary accomplishment following another.

In 1957, when some nationally known surgeons had succeeded in stopping a patient's heart during an operation and starting it again after making repairs; when the flow of blood actually was slowed down in accordance with the surgeon's advanced plan; when high standards of safety demanded one doctor per 2,000 civilians; when 20 per cent of the world's medical men were practicing in this country, news announcements were numerous concerning surgical advances. One was to the effect that the replacement of a damaged heart is within the realm of possibility. Making it known was Dr. Edgar F. Berman of Baltimore's Sinai Hospital, who with two associates, performed a heart-replacement operation from one dog to another.

The heart was completely isolated. It was transposed to another dog. Then it initiated its own beat and sustained the circulation of the host for two hours.

In the development of ways to replace a heart in man, this operation was heralded as another milestone along the road of imagination, bravery, and practical experimentation. It was to be followed by another daring experiment, that of the selective cooling of the brain to 65 degrees to enable surgeons to stop circulation over 15 minutes while the heart is opened and repaired.

In 1957, when membership in the State Medical Society totaled 3370, with the most aggressive H. E. Kasten of Beloit following in the presidential footsteps of that great leader L. O. Simenstad of Osceola, new advances were in the Society's overall plans. One concerned an unparalleled post-graduate educational opportunity for physicians who must guide their patients through an increasingly complex field of medical care.

Heart specialists were saying that science slowly is removing the shrouds of mystery from heart disease, that polio can be conquered through Salk vaccine, that an amazing lag had been evident throughout the country in the usage of Salk vaccine.

At the same time, the total number of mental cases in the nation was approximately 750,000. Alcoholics totaled 4,000,000. The number, authorities said, was increasing gradually. The problems of disability and mental illness caused by alcohol were challenges which the public wasn't meeting successfully. A broader program of information, education, and crusade was under way. Fund-raising campaigns for heart, cancer, tuberculosis, polio, and palsy research organizations were well directed everywhere.

All in all, as this cavalcade of history keeps rolling on, the miracles of modern medicine are keeping America strong. Life is being prolonged. Each miracle is helping modern medicine to lengthen the average American's span of life. Since the discovery of penicillin, physician successes have been enormous.

The wonder story of penicillin began in 1928 when Sir Alexander Fleming of England investigated a mould and discovered one of the greatest germ killers in history. Again it was obvious that, whenever the right man and the right circumstances are linked together, a new discovery is made.

One startling medical announcement follows another. Hospital stays are shorter. Safety in surgery is on the increase. It has improved all the operations and has made possible many new ones.

Since 1946, authorities say, some operations have become 20 per cent safer, others from 50 to 70 per cent, due chiefly to specializations in the field of anaesthesiology, which have increased the surgeons' skill. Other important factors include the improved hospital service, with recovery rooms for post-surgical patients, better use of blood for patients in surgery, specialized knowledge concerning secretions and full utilization of it, immediate care of the patient in preparation for the operation.

Surgeons today are bold. As time goes on, they will be getting bolder. The miracle of anaesthesia, which offers greater safety to the patient, is putting more courage into the surgeons' daily work. Without this wonderful progress in anaesthesia, a great many operations could not be accomplished.

As a result of this recent progress, the days of World War I seem dark when compared with today. In the Navy during World War I, approximately seven per cent of the wounded men died, many of them of shock or infection or both. One half of the compound-fracture cases were permanently crippled, and 12 per cent of them resulted in death.

During World War II, when 28 states had a dangerous shortage of doctors, with one third of the nation's doctors in active military service, death took not more than one per cent of the Navy's wounded men. Only ten per cent of those wounded were disabled. As for the sea fighters suffering from abdominal wounds, there were only five deaths in every 100 cases, compared with 20 deaths during World War I.

Further research in the military field brings forth a repository of interesting facts concerning medical and dental progress.

In the early days of our country, for example, dental service for military personnel was non-existent. Until the war between states, fighters on land and sea had no dentists to go to when suffering from decayed or ulcerated teeth. Dentistry was strictly a private business, not a responsibility of government; and if a soldier with a painful tooth asked another man in his regiment to perform an extraction with a pair of pliers, there was no regulation to prevent it.

In the Confederate army during an early stage, one could pay for dental treatment, and the fee for a single gold filling was equal to a private's pay for six months.

Later, in 1864, the congress of the Confederacy passed a law for the conscription of dentists into their ranks. That was the first time in United States history when a military man could receive free dental service.

The war ended, dentistry was forgotten. Not until 1901 was it revived. A bill in congress then insured the employment of dental surgeons on a contract basis for both officers and enlisted men. Seven years later a dental corps became a part of the army's medical department.

Like other army organizations, the Dental Corps has had a history of ups and downs. Their problems often have paralleled those of other army segments. After the second world war, for instance, when all segments were demobilizing and disposing of surplus equipment and supplies, the Dental Corps had on hand nearly 60,000 sets of unneeded false teeth.

It all is a reminder of a comical and indecent incident which happened after a battle in Texas, where Sam Houston's forces were fighting Mexicans. One of Houston's men pulled teeth with pliers from dead Mexican jaws, placing them in a bucket, selling 'em later as souvenirs at $5 apiece.

Again, in matters relating to public health, our medical men cannot eliminate death or disease. They only can alter the cause and prolong life.

In 1958 many diseases remained undefeated. One was polio. A visit to any hospital-polio clinic shows that the deadly crippler is leaving much work to be finished. It's a story of braces, crutches, therapy, treatment, exercises, new equipment, further examinations, uncertainty.

In efforts to obtain the broadest-possible results in the 1957 campaign against polio, the Council of the State Medical Society endorsed a plan to inoculate all persons under age 40 in every county with Salk vaccine. Similar action was taken by other states.

A century ago, when Indians of North Wisconsin were defenseless in their struggles against smallpox, with no medical care and no vaccine to help them, people in white communities being served by doctors were able to immunize themselves by way of Jenner's smallpox vaccine. At that time the epidemic form of infantile paralysis was unknown. The first reported outbreak, in 1887, was in Sweden.

In this country in 1916, polio hit hard, spreading through 27 states, with a total of 27,363 cases. Its toll nationally during the next 15 years was heavy; and until 1954, when nearly two million school children were inoculated with Salk vaccine, the most fatal form of polio known as bulbospinal was threatening to create vast perils. Too, the drug market was offering no cure for this horrible disease.

What a difference time makes!

During the 19th century, when polio was not a perilous Wisconsin health factor, cholera, smallpox, diphtheria, and typhoid fever were ruthless epidemics, striking from one generation to another. The fight to get them under control was long, tedious, and discouraging, seemingly hopeless at times, with tuberculosis also frightening the populace at large.

Negligent public officials in some places virtually were agents of plague. In Milwaukee, for example, people were permitted to drink impure water in spite of warnings by medical men that an alarming spread of typhoid fever locally could be traced to the contaminated Milwaukee River.

Then one day in 1880, when thousands of dead fish were seen floating on water poisoned by sewage, caustic critics of the press demanded that the incapable Water Board members be ousted and then replaced by competent defenders of the public health.

In time, Milwaukeeans were not drinking polluted water. The dangers of typhoid fever were vastly reduced. Members of the State Medical Society kept preaching the importance of sanitation. With better drugs, wider knowledge, gradually-improved techniques, and stronger loyalty to cause, these immortal men of medicine finally had all old epidemics under control.

In 1957, when observing the Society's 116th year of existence, Council members were doing their best to ward off as many polio attacks as possible through vaccination. They also were conducting surveys in many fields, including hospitalization, with its never-ending spiraling of costs; and to determine just what the Wisconsin medical profession at large could do to provide assistance in stabilizing various cost elements, the Council assigned that vital project to the Foundation. At the same time it set aside $10,000 for use by the Foundation in this special work.

As a further challenge for men of vision, the State Medical Society early in '57 broadened its responsibilities in civil defense. It appraised military needs and made known to interns and hospital authorities everywhere that physicians who accept residency appointments would be doing so at their own risk.

Being sought regularly is a well-developed program of staff conferences in hospitals for the purpose of discussing maternal deaths and special hazards of obstetrics. Local review of fetal and neonatal deaths, too, is encouraged, along with a vision-screening program in schools, aid for crippled children, and a more vigorous campaign against cancer quackery in the state.

Concerning quackery, the Committee said:

> The recent action of the Food and Drug Administration in warning the public against the so-called Hoxsey treatment is commended and endorsed. The Committee urges the appropriate medical authorities everywhere to take similar steps to end further deception in the future.
>
> All members of the State Medical Society are requested to cooperate in a survey and a study to expose cancer quackery in Wisconsin. These efforts will be conducted along sound legal lines, so as to assure protection of the physician-patient relationship.

These special Committee statements indicate that a courageous and forceful campaign against the agents of fallacy is essential for the public welfare. They imply a contemplated survey of Wisconsin physicians to acquire specific information concerning the activities of quacks and cultists, with a view of exposing facts previously unpublished. Results of each survey will be used to develop an educational program for physicians and the public.

Meanwhile, committeemen of this powerful state organization are continuing to attend informal meetings of the Board of Health. They are holding health conferences in schools, and are ever ready to attend special meetings called by the American Medical Association, as well as the North Central Conference, which has for its membership the active medical leaders of Iowa, Minnesota, the Dakotas, Nebraska, and Wisconsin.

Problems each year are becoming broader in scope. They include those of hospital administration and the hospitals' relation to the public. According to a joint 1957 report of the Committee on Hospital Relationships and the Council on Medical Service, the tremendous growth and use of hospitals in recent years have made these problems more complex.

BELOIT'S DR. H. E. KASTEN

whose presidential term in State Medical Society signified a progress which no other state could excel.

OSCEOLA'S DR. L. O. SIMENSTAD

whose state-wide medical leadership long pointed to Upper Wisconsin's prestige.

Virtually the work of Wisconsin's tireless medical society is of mammoth proportions as it continues to prove that the heritage of medicine is truly grand, and that, in the one huge overall project of upholding the old dignity and prestige, it must point to the ever pressing need for more active medical communities. Indeed, by its achievement since early territorial days, it has demonstrated immense value in public-health problems everywhere.

In 1932, when this organization published a detailed outline of industrial-health accomplishments by physicians and nurses throughout Wisconsin, the resultant publicity benefits were of value in other states. Wisconsin actually was the first state to make known a broad industrial program of this kind.

A most recent issue of *Occupational Health — a Guide for Physicians and Nurses in Industry*, published by the Council on Medical Service, shows the changing concept of industrial health. It recommends full or part-time medical service in even the small industrial plants.

The current scope of our state society's public-information service is partly indicated in the following 1957 report: Approximately 2,000 copies of *Careers in Health* were given to high-school students, and more than 28,000 copies of health literature were distributed to county agents, homemakers, 4-H club members, and others; 350 establishments in business and industry received health-education articles monthly for their bulletin boards and house publications; 73 radio stations each month made "spot" announcements concerning health advice; 39 radio stations, as a public service, regularly gave 15-minute programs called *The March of Medicine*, with the listeners reasonably estimated at 300,000 per week.

More than 1,000 inquiries from *March of Medicine* listeners were received by Dr. Robert C. Parkin, assistant to the dean, University of Wisconsin Medical School, who serves as director for that special radio feature; 700 tape-recorded programs on 10 health topics were sent to 72 high schools for classroom teaching; an estimated 50,000 persons viewed the Society's Healthland exhibit during the 1956 Wisconsin State Fair; a minimum of 10,000 column inches of space were used by daily newspapers in 75 different releases;

there were 450 requests from physicians for loan packets, literature, and medical-society guides; 55 students of high school and college received loan packets containing medical and economic subjects; 26 articles were written for *Wisconsin Agriculturist and Farmer* which serves 200,000 farm families.

More than 2,000 persons requested copies of *March of Medicine* programs; a television series, lasting for 13 weeks, produced by the State Medical Society, was presented by five TV stations; 34 one-year subscriptions to the magazine *Today's Health* were awarded to 4-H clubs with outstanding health projects; various other Society services, particularly those of lecture and exhibit, were productive of good results.

Of the problems being studied and discussed regularly by the Council on Medical Service, nursing education is foremost, with many challenges. It concerns an acute shortage of nurses and makes necessary a state-wide survey, a long series of reports and meetings, which involve the State Board of Nursing, the State Department of Vocational and Adult Education, hospital authorities, and school heads as well as the sponsoring State Medical Society members.

Another problem, regarded as serious by critics everywhere, concerns voluntary organizations outside of the medical profession which, in lacking liaison with medical men, have been actively engaged in cases of mental disorders.

True, these well-meaning public workers have set good goals for themselves, seeking to make what they feel are worthwhile contributions to health-improvement enterprises; but as long as these volunteers stay aloof from medical men and keep doing things which licensed doctors cannot endorse, they should start recognizing society's safe standards — those leading or primary principles which our general public has as a guide.

Surely there are enough signs outside of the zodiac pointing to the reasons why an unalert, improperly trained, public health worker should see Society's guide posts and the principles upon which formalized behavior is built. Yet when misguided aggressiveness is powered by a variety of hazards, including ultra-ego, certain goals must be achieved.

A critical public, however, is aware that the direction of activities relating to neurological cases essentially is a responsibility of duly qualified authorities in the fields of medicine and public health.

In recent years, while dealing with mental-health problems, disseminating information and otherwise seeking to motivate preventive measures through education, the State Medical Society has held conferences in many schools, with parents, teachers, physicians, dentists, nurses, and public health workers giving strong support. In efforts to add much more impetus to this program, the spearheading state organization is urging all county units to sponsor a series of conferences and lectures at appropriate intervals for the citizenry at large.

As time rolls on, the morbidness of tuberculosis is being placed in the proper focus. Facilities for use in case finding must be increased if this disease of the lung is to be conquered. State health laws, too, demand more strength.

Thus far the pasteurization of milk has been the biggest single achievement in reducing the spread of tubercular germs; and as an indication of further progress in the field of discovery, two milk-pasteurization processes are currently in common use. In one, named for Scientist Louis Pasteur, the milk is heated to not lower than 143 degrees. It is kept there at least 30 minutes and promptly cooled to 50 degrees or lower. This process destroys any harmful bacteria that may be evident without affecting flavor and food value. The other method raises the temperature quickly to at least 160 degrees and holds it there at least 15 seconds, followed by rapid cooling.

Modern discoveries are blessings vast in scope. With each new one, the story of disease is shortened considerably.

Outstanding is the recent discovery by Maurice R. Hilleman, supervisory bacteriologist at Walter Reed Army Medical Center in Washington, D. C., who has found a new group of viruses which are responsible for such diseases as pneumonia, colds, grippe, and acute sore throat.

As a result of this great work, an opportunity has been created for the medical profession to conduct research toward the development of a suitable vaccine for use on man in combating these dreaded afflictions.

A single vaccine for colds, flu, and polio was the early 1958 aim of Tulane University doctors, who opened the way for a multiple-purpose vaccine by proving that influenza virus may be grown in monkey kidney-tissue cultures, the same method used for polio vaccine.

The doctors at Tulane said they had isolated a new virus which causes colds. They also pointed out that scientists eventually will have to face the question of whether there is a limit to the number or type of viruses that can be added to a vaccine and still get an antibody response.

Multi-purpose injections, said the announcement, might save both time and money as well as providing some protection.

Doctor Herman Bundesen, of Chicago, for decades a leading spokesman in the American Medical Association, recently put emphasis on the need for a vaccine to protect us all from virus pneumonia.

"Even though virus pneumonia is seldom fatal," Bundesen said, *"it usually does put its victim in bed with subsequent loss of time from work. At least 17 different viruses, ultramicroscopic in size and extremely difficult to indentify, may cause pneumonia. Generally, by the time we could identify the virus which has struck the person, he or she would be either well or dead."*

Going to bed and calling your doctor, Bundesen says, is one of the best protections against virus pneumonia. A simple cold comes first. In its fourth or fifth day, virus pneumonia begins insidiously. It seeks to cause chilliness, a severe headache, a fever varying from 100 to 103 degrees, and loss of appetite. For several days the cough will remain dry and tight. Finally the coughing produces a thin, watery sputum which may be streaked with blood.

Why develop a condition of this kind when it so easily can be prevented through quick medical care?

Once the habits have been placed in a mold of concrete, it is almost impossible to chisel 'em out?

New techniques in heart surgery, developed by Dr. Walter Lillehie and his group at the University of Minnesota, are being used successfully by surgeons in other places, more particularly the Fitzsimmons Army Hospital in Denver.

There, Dr. John M. Salyer reports, the new methods are resulting in the correction of congenital malformations and defects. They allow by-passing the heart and lungs. In this way, surgeons open heart chambers for direct vision, evaluation, and correction of specific heart defects.

"This method," said the noted Army surgeon, "has been made possible by the use of the extra-corporal or extra-body technique. That is, use of mechanical equipment which takes over the functions of the heart and lungs to allow the surgery."

Dr. Salyer mentions an electric pump, which does the heart's job of circulating blood through the body, and a disposable plastic oxygenator which continues to oxygenate the desaturated blood and removes carbon dioxide. The electric pump can be used for as long as 70 minutes.

Studies of the human heart are continuing to reveal many new enlightening facts. At a conference of scientists held recently in Milwaukee, sponsored by the Marquette Medical School, Dr. Lucien A. Brouha of E. I. du Pont de Nemours and Company pointed out that a worker in a hot, humid environment uses far more energy to fight the heat than he expends on his or her job.

He said the studies showed that the hearts of normal workers took longer to recover from physical effort in high temperatures. He advises that supervisors and foremen in all work places could get higher efficiency and better morale by scheduling fewer rest periods when the temperature is about 60, and more when it approaches 100.

Management is negative when it permits heat to take more energy than the job, Dr. Brouha said. It is stupid to give workers that kind of environment. It pays for 25 percent physical labor—the job assignment—and 75 percent for internal labor to meet the heat stress.

Throughout the country, management would do well to recognize these facts and to adopt new measures designed to improve. Their places of manufacturing would realize bigger net profits and their workers would cultivate a friendlier attitude if men in the front offices would accept some sound hints from the nation's top medical experts.

Doctors everywhere keep warning that heart disorders are being acquired by adults regularly as the result of harmful work conditions. Congenital heart cases are being studied by nationally-prominent physicians, who also are pointing out that, as the outgrowth of American medical achievements highlighted lately by work on the heart, many congenital malformations of the heart and circulatory system are now curable by surgery.

Lingering long in retrospect should be the statements made recently by Dr. Paul R. Hawley, director of the American College of Surgeons, who, in a special article written for International News Service, stated that each day now approximately 25,000 men, women, and children are being wheeled into the operating rooms of our nation's hospitals, anesthetized, and operated upon.

More than nine million were destined to be operated upon in 1959. Their health, and in a great number of cases their lives, were to be entrusted to the surgeon's knowledge and skill, and above all, his judgment.

Almost daily we read about new operations, improved techniques, better care for patients everywhere. Operations on the human heart keep increasing in number. Courageous surgeons keep showing almost incredible skill. They work in teams. Anesthetists, pathologists, radiologists, biophysicists, biochemists, and nursing specialists all collaborate together in the operating room, where a pump-oxygenator performs the combined work of the heart and lungs, maintaining vital circulation while the by-passed heart is being operated upon.

All in all, God is at work here.

Another mechanical marvel of our time is the artificial kidney, an apparatus which takes over kidney functions during an operation.

As for other disclosures made recently by nationally-prominent specialists, the one concerning new drugs for mental patients and for those who have a mild emotional disorder is of vital interest everywhere. In preliminary tests thus far, these drugs have been showing encouragement, according to researchers in psychiatry at Tulane University.

There is earnest advice in statements recently voiced by the government's leading research specialist in the field of tranquilizer drugs—Dr. Robert Felix, director of the National Research Institute of Mental Health, which is a noted center for the U. S. Public Health Service at Bethesda, Md.

"Be mighty careful about tranquilizer drugs," warns Dr. Felix.

They can be harmful. Dangerous addictions may be the result.

Tranquilizers never should be used unless prescribed by a doctor, and such prescriptions should be non-refillable, said Dr. Felix. They are not cures. They can be of great value in effecting cures, but actually they do not cure or alter the fundamental disorder.

With medical progress on the march, our State Medical Society continues to study the problems of neglected and crippled children, of maternal mortality, of mental patients discharged from mental institutions, with tuberculosis a lingering threat.

Continued health examinations are being stressed in schools as a protection against communicable diseases. This factor is dominant in the control of tuberculosis. Currently this case load throughout the state is not heavy, lower than the 1956 total, which was 217, with most of the cases properly isolated, so as to avoid spread.

All of Wisconsin's 157 hospitals licensed for maternity service answered the State Society's most recent questionnaire concerning maternity records.

Incidentally, have you been doing your part in helping the State Medical Society to achieve its fund-raising goal, preparatory to the restoration of the Fort Crawford Military Hospital at Prairie du Chien?

To complete this project, making it a monument to the immortal contributions of Wisconsin medical men, the sponsors need state-wide help.

As we all go onward to grave and eternal life, with our Fort Crawford shrine serving as a reminder of the blessings received by us through a great medical profession, the government of Wisconsin continues to stand out as a potent force in health education.

Prevention of disease is its never-ending theme, and its chief exponent in the capitol is Dr. Carl N. Neupert, Health Officer, who has followed in the wake of Cornelius A. Harper, venerable pioneer and public servant, whose rise from a farm boy's status at Hazel Green to that of preeminence in medicine at the capitol should encourage the poorest of present-day farm boys to scale the achievement heights.

Neupert, like Harper, is focusing his attention on health hazards; and in one of his latest releases to the newspapers, he said that approximately a million residents of this country probably have diabetes and don't know it.

"It is important," he said, *"that these people be found as soon as possible and helped. Otherwise their uncontrolled diabetes may result in other hazards, such as impaired sight, kidney disease, and premature hardening of the arteries."*

Diabetes is a disorder caused by a deficiency of insulin in the body. Insulin, a hormone produced by a gland called the pancreas, makes it possible for the sugars and starches in food we eat to be used by the body to provide energy.

"In a diabetic person," Dr. Neupert said, *"the pancreas is not producing enough insulin. Hence, some or most of the sugars and starches eaten by the person with diabetes are neither used for energy nor stored for future use. They pile up, causing an excess of sugar in the blood."*

Diabetes can be controlled by diet and insulin treatment, advises Neupert. The earlier it is found, the easier it is to control. People who have diabetes can live essentially normal lives if their condition is not neglected.

Tests for this disease are simple. It takes a doctor only a few minutes to analyze a sample of urine or blood.

Since the release by Dr. Neupert of this information concerning the early discovery of diabetes through a timely physical examination, there was a surprising news story for diabetics.

Diabetics were told by the Upjohn scientists of Kalamazoo that a new pill may free a very large number of them from lifelong slavery to the hypodermic needle.

The new pill is called tolbutamide. It was given by 400 different doctors to 7,000 or more patients throughout the country in tests sponsored by the scientists of Kalamazoo.

In approximately 76 percent of these cases, involving the age groups between twenty and eighty, the responses proved to be good or excellent, the official report said.

One of the persons tested was a New Yorker of 79, who, as a diabetic for 55 years, had given himself 10,000 or more injections of insulin. The new drug worked so well for him that he discarded his hypodermic needle. No longer does he disinfect the skin on his thigh, jab a needle into his flesh, inject the insulin, and with fear, await the reaction, each time hoping the dose would not result in shock or in a diabetic coma.

Under tolbutamide treatment for eighteen months, when no insulin was given, this patient was under control. His urine tests were negative. His blood-sugar levels were down to normal. Still a diabetic, he took on new life. His tablets symbolized a half-century dream coming true.

During the long period of tolbutamide-test treatments, informants of the American Diabetes Association were pointing out the fallacies of premature optimism, saying there was no certainty the new chemicals soon would replace insulin injections.

In statements made shortly thereafter by doctors who were conducting the tests, it was disclosed that, in the age group between twenty and forty, tolbutamide had proved successful in one case out of three. More encouraging was a subsequent report, showing success in Germany, where the new compound had been lowering blood sugar in the majority of middle-aged and elderly diabetics.

During the test period in one section of this country, each of 120 patients consumed more than a pound of the white tablets. At the same time, some physicians were saying there was no way to predict whether a patient might or might not continue to benefit from the tablets for periods of five, ten, or twenty years. Quite obvious was an attitude of cautious enthusiasm.

One scientist said the new drug cannot work unless at least some insulin is present. He emphasized that it cannot cure diabetes, and that it must be taken indefinitely. Dietary control is still essential.

"As a result of great scientific achievements," he said, "our people may be upon the threshold of a new era of therapy in diabetes, for they give promise that a significant portion of our diabetic population may be unshackled from syringe and needle."

This statement, another symbol of medicine's new golden age, shows the value of teamwork in our medical profession. New ideas, new words, new discoveries keep developing the teamwork to higher levels of efficiency and success. So life expectancy (from birth) is one of the cheerful topics of this day. During the period of 1945 to 1958, it increased from 65 to 70 years. While it was implying a steadfast trend upward, doctors throughout our nation were prolonging life for approximately 1,240,000 citizens who, if deprived of the new treatments, suddenly would have ended their lives here on earth.

Persons saved from early death through timely and successful medical research have been naming their pills "Happy." Druggists have been pointing out that three out of four prescriptions written today are for drugs unknown prior to World War II.

Ulcer sufferers are being promised relief by way of a pill which soothes the ulcer itself. The manufacturer refers to it as "split-level" therapy in the treatment of gastro-intestinal disorders.

Incidentally, in seeking to protect your health, have you been keeping tension at a minimum? Are you able to relax under pressure?

Undoubtedly you know that prolonged anxiety and emotional tension make the membranes of the stomach irritable, engorged, inflamed, and liable to tiny abrasions, and that these openings are attacked by harsh gastric juices which have been known to develop full-scale ulcers in as little as four days.

Has the common cold been tantalizing you?

You, too, have had long membership in what could be termed the Amalgamated Order of Cold Catchers?

Medical science, in full sympathy with you, is predicting the development of a strong defense.

Dr. Winston H. Price, of Johns Hopkins School of Hygiene and Public Health, has isolated this virus and has made the first successful vaccine against the demon cold. Its effectiveness was tested in a controlled sample involving approximately 400 volunteers. It is described as the first true cold virus ever to be isolated.

Prior to mass production of the vaccine, Dr. Price said, more extensive tests were necessary. During the trial tests, the vaccine was effective in 80 percent of cases of colds caused by what is known as the JH virus—a virus believed to be responsible for 30 percent of the colds caught by human beings.

While focusing attention on these latest discoveries, authorities were pointing out that, during the ten-year period of 1947-1957, more was achieved in the field of medicine than in the previous 50 years.

That's only the beginning. Researchers steadily are drawing closer to hidden facts concerning persistent ailments. One reminder is in a drug company's release to medical doctors of an anti-arthritis chemical called chloroquine. It is said to attack the disease itself rather than just its symptoms. Reversing the disease safely is the intent of this drug—a great blessing for sufferers of arthritis.

Never before in history has the medical profession's war on the agents of ill health been so intense. To help prove it, the Veterans Administration in Washington recently announced the discovery of a new anticoagulant that may be of value in treating heart-and-blood-vessel diseases.

"Drugs now used to prevent blood clotting," VA officials said, *"can cause undesirable reactions unless rigid precautions are taken."*

The VA said its new substance may be of a type that will not produce these undesirable reactions.

Heart disease, still the leading cause of death in this country, killed more than 840,000 persons in 1956; and while making known his sentiments concerning this statistical report, Dr. Jeremiah Stamler, investigator for the American Heart Association, said the habitual diet is a decisive factor responsible for heart disease.

Many Americans eat too much, he told a writer of *Town and Country* magazine. They eat too much fat, particularly of the saturated variety; they eat too many carbohydrates, fats, and starches, empty-calorie foods that are high in calories and low in nutrition and bulk, Dr. Stamler said. Our diets are unbalanced, with too many calories in proportion to nutrients.

Just how do we insure balance?

According to that scientist who knows, we should stop adding fats to so many foods by frying meats, dressing salads with mayonnaise, putting butter on vegetables. We should serve fruit for desert. Breakfast habit should be modified. It is best to eat fruit and whole-grain cereals and bread instead of the traditional bacon and eggs, known for a huge caloric intake of saturated fat. At other meals, we are advised, we should eat lean meats. Don't fry them or add heavy sauces or gravies!

In connection with the subject of heart attack, there is enlightenment in knowledge that a group of researchers headed by Dr. George L. Curran of Kansas Medical School is working on a new preventive approach. New discoveries, with a promise of safe anti-rust drugs, are indicated in late progress reports.

Heart attacks, specialists tell us, are the result of heart arteries becoming narrowed or clogged with fatty deposits much like rust inside a water pipe.

Anti-rust drugs, researchers feel, would dissolve out some of the fatty accumulation or prevent it from forming, so as to keep the blood pipelines open. Such drugs would be a tremendous boon to thousands of persons who already have had a heart attack, or who are unconsciously destined for one.

While Kansas doctors keep working on their momentous drug project, surgeons around the country are continuing to mend hearts.

At El Paso, Texas, a delicate heart operation recently was performed on a little girl to permit her to live a healthy, normal life. At Madison, Wis., seven surgeons participated in an hours-long operation to mend a hole in a little boy's heart. In order to maintain blood circulation while the condition was being corrected, these surgeons used a mechanical heart.

Cases go on, usually in a very humble, dignified, unheralded way, as this amazing era of medical accomplishment keeps itself geared to the vast potentialities of the future. Another life is saved; another family is held together. Opportunities for worthy-public contributions are again offered to those who emerge from the hospitals sound of body and mind.

The U. S. Public Health Service offers encouragement in a statement that, of every ten persons who have a stroke, only one now will be left completely helpless. Nine out of ten stroke patients can be taught to walk again. Three out of ten can learn to do gainful work.

As helpful information for those who sustain a stroke, the Public Health Service points out the following:

Soon after the stroke has occurred, action should be started to help restore the use of the affected arm and leg. This begins with massage and assisted movements of the arm and leg.

Within a few days, the patient is encouraged to move his own arm and leg. Gradually he learns to sit up, to stand, to finally walk.

The physician may instruct the family how they can help with some of the procedures. Assistance may be needed from some one with a special training in this work—a physical therapist.

From the beginning, it is important that the patient's family have an encouraging, hopeful attitude. The patient should be included as much in family life and in planning for his own care.

Re-training muscles and speech after a stroke often is a long, difficult process, but the accomplishment in being able to care for one's own needs is most rewarding.

In past years there was little that doctors could do for patients who had strokes. Today we have a much more hopeful attitude, as reflected in the foregoing statements. There are a number of things that can be done to help patients immediately after a stroke has occurred.

Just what is a stroke?

It occurs when an artery to a part of the brain ruptures or is closed by a blood clot; and a person who has had a stroke may have paralysis of an arm and leg. He also may have difficulty in speaking. Once in a while, these symptoms clear up rather quickly, but frequently some physical disability remains.

As we all keep facing these hazards of health, medical science moves along with a progress that is steady.

Doctor Edward A. Banner, assistant professor of obstetrics and gynecology at the Mayo Clinic in Rochester, Minn., for example, tells how a general practitioner examining a woman in his own office can detect cancer before it is visible to the human eye.

"A recently developed method," Dr. Banner said during a meeting of the Southwestern Medical Association in El Paso, "will discover a malignancy in the cervic in an average of one out of every 150 women."

This new diagnostic technique, he said, can detect cancer on an average of eight years before the growth is visible.

Cancers discovered at this early stage generally can be cured 100 percent, Dr. Banner asserted.

In describing the new method, he said the doctor takes a papanicolaou smear from his patient. This smear can and should be taken in any physician's office as a matter of routine.

"If it appears that malignant cells are present in the smear," Dr. Banner explained, "small pieces of the patient's tissue should be examined in the laboratories of a trained pathologist to confirm the diagnosis.

"If and when the diagnosis obtained from the smear is confirmed, then the cure of the cancer is undertaken and, because it is in such an early stage, the cure virtually is always successful.

Experiments to improve the techniques of using the papanicolaou smear have been conducted at the Mayo Clinic for many years.

In keeping with this consistently effective trend of experimentation throughout our country, one enlightening news item follows another. Medical men profit from them. Patients, in turn, reap the benefits. Barriers to healthy aging are being overcome gradually.

Lost hearing is being restored. New skin-grafting techniques are reconstructing the destroyed portions of eardrum and middle ear. Similar methods are used in closing a perforation in the eardrum. Group therapy is proving effective in treatment of mental illness. Mothers are trained for childbirth.

A surgeon from Japan makes known that, in repairing a heart, he had cooled a patient's brain to 65 degrees, stopping circulation for nearly fifteen minutes. This method, which combines drugs and artificial cooling, was introduced years ago by Dr. Henri Laborit of Paris and is now being used widely as an operative procedure.

The cavalcade of progress keeps moving onward. Garden clubs, determined to help reduce hay-fever cases to a minimum, are conducting city-wide drives against weeds. Smokers are punching pinholes near the mouthpiece of cigarette, reducing the content of tar—a causative factor in lung cancer.

Our nation's 5,000 entomologists, who study the lives, habits, and control of insects, are urging an all-out, swat-the-fly campaign. College heads are studying the suggestion that prospective teachers be given a health-education subject along with their regular course. A team headed by Dr. R. Frederick Becker of Duke University continues to study a cause-and-effect link between the anesthetic or sedatives given at childbirth and the affliction known as cerebral palsy. Progress in anesthesia now includes visits by anesthetists before an operation, new drugs to relieve anxiety and tension, more skillful use of the improved drugs.

While a cigarette advertiser continues to point out the kindness which his product gives to each smoker's throat, spokesmen for cancer-research institutes keep releasing factual information concerning tobacco harm.

According to Dr. Ernest L. Wynder of the Sloan-Ketting Institute for Cancer Research in New York, smokers of pipe and cigar have a higher incidence of cancer higher up in the respiratory tract.

This latest study is based on 209 men with cancer of the larynx, 209 men of the same age free of cancer, 132 men with lung cancer, 542 men with cancer of the oral cavity, and 207 patients who had either non-cancerous sores of the head, neck, or chest, or cancers of the lower gastro-intestinal region.

Cancer-causing agents, Dr. Wynder said, include heavy drinking plus heavy smoking and a man who consistently takes seven or more shots of hard liquor a day is regarded as a heavy drinker.

Men who combine heavy drinking with heavy smoking actually are running ten times the risk of cancer of the larynx, or voicebox, or mouth than heavy smokers who drink moderately or not at all.

Currently being analyzed for conclusive data in New York are the heavy beer and wine drinkers.

The approximate number of Americans killed by lung cancer annually is 25,000, the U. S. Public Health Service declares. Excessive cigarette smoking is one of the causes.

Another fact worth remembering is that throat irritation or "tobacco cough" from heavy smoking can create a hazard during surgery.

Anesthesiologists say a patient of this kind can develop coughing spasms when given anesthesia, or painful coughing spells later. Patients scheduled for surgery should be advised not to smoke for a whole week prior to entering the hospital.

Selfish advertisers of finely-cut tobacco enclosed in thin paper do not offer such helpful hints to their smoking public. They do not point out that, after a prolonged study of the smoking habits of nearly 190,000 men in the age groups 50 to 70, the American Cancer Society views heavy cigarette smoking as one certain way to shorten life.

All of which prompts the question, when did you last have a medical doctor examine you?

You are so healthy you do not need an examination?

Years ago in Superior a railroader said: "Since my boyhood, I haven't needed a doctor. I'm never sick, and why spend money when you know you are okay?"

A month later this sage of hygiene was in a hospital, rushed there in an ambulance as the result of an alarm expressed by his wife. An operation revealed a cancer.

"*I kill all of my germs with whiskey,*" a Chequamegon Bay longshoreman once told a merchant friend.

True it was. This staunch friend of the bottle for many years had been averaging one pint of whiskey daily. On Sunday, near his bed, he had in easy access what he called his "snops" while neighbors were on the way to church. Surely he drank his "snops" straight. He didn't need water or ginger ale as a chaser.

What finally happened to him? In what shape was he when entering eternal life?

High blood pressure had cut him down. His lungs showed massive pulmonary fat emboli in the large vascular channels. His various ailments plainly indicated that, in his life here on earth, his plan to destroy himself had been thorough and long range.

As self destruction continues to be a definitely fixed, human factor, the strong men of medicine keep coming on from one generation to another, easing pain, combating disease, restoring lost health, giving others an opportunity to take part in worthwhile enterprises, increasing the average span of life.

To further illustrate their progress, let us consider the following news releases as 1958 was starting to unfold:

Infant deaths will be reduced considerably as a result of the improved care of mothers. Generally throughout the country, the health of mothers is being improved; and as obstetricians become better trained, conditions of labor and pregnancy are getting better. More progress is being made in the action to improve the condition of the body and its environment before birth.

A New York doctor says he uses a variation of television's sleep-inducing powers to prepare children for surgery. This idea works so well that an operation actually can be fun for youngsters, especially in the age group of nine to fourteen. Dr. Albert M. Betcher of Albert Einstein Medical College tells about it in his lectures.

Mrs. Lou Gehrig, wife of the immortal Yankee ballplayer, national campaign chairman of Muscular Dystrophy Associations of America, now heads hundreds of thousands of volunteers who call on their neighbors in the nation-wide drive for funds.

In Wisconsin, where the United Cerebral Palsy Association has made commendable headway in its particular field, health crusaders are being cheered. Recently at Northland College, for instance, a seminar conducted by the United Cerebral-Palsy group was marked by the personal appearances of Karl York, St. Luke's Hospital administrator, Racine; Dr. Elden Bond, Milwaukee; Dr. Earl Speicher, secretary of the Northern Wisconsin group; and Sherwood A. Messner, New York, director of UCPA program services.

Amazing is this recent announcement by Dr. Oscar Creech, Jr., of the American Medical Association: "Synthetic blood-vessel grafts are proving equally as satisfactory as human-artery grafts in 'detour' operations to alleviate hardening of the arteries.

"Rather than treat the blocked segment, we merely bypass it with a synthetic graft in what is known as a detour operation. The results have been good," said Dr. Creech, whose status in the department of surgery at Tulane University School of Medicine is that of chairman.

If ever a puissant group of medical historians in this country collaborate diligently for a decade or so in producing the full scope of these recent achievements, many volumes will enslave a conscientious reader for several months.

City, county, and state health officers, meanwhile, will do their best to help the process of education. For example, in the People's Forum of the Ashland Daily Press appeared this advice from Dr. C. A. Grand:

> We are entering the season of the year when the incident of acute infectious, "colds" are prevalent. These infections spread from person to person by droplets —that is, the sick person coughs or sneezes without covering the mouth, disseminates the droplets with organisms into his neighbor's nose or mouth. After a short incubation period, this neighbor becomes ill. Thus, disease spreads from person to person.
>
> School children are young and have little immunity. Thus they are susceptible to infections. Some ride in crowded buses for many miles, increasing the exposure to a sick fellow student. One such student infects the whole bus.
>
> To assist in controlling the spread of acute infections (colds), especially since the Asian Influenza came in to spread its peril, it is important that parents of sick children do not send them to school until they have recovered.

From Dallas, Texas, the Associated Press said, "The Board of Medical Examiners has sought a permanent injunction to prevent Harry Hoxsey from practicing medicine. The Board asked a judgment against Hoxsey by District Judge Charles Long."

The Texas medical board should be saluted everywhere by the advocates of critical standards. Better yet, letters of compliment should be sent to the board chairman in a manner which denotes wide public acclaim.

At Denver, Colorado, the district office of the U. S. Food and Drug Administration warned that housewives and consumers should beware of exaggerated claims of fallacious salesmen who go from house to house soliciting orders for so-called food supplements. In this warning it was pointed out that our American food supply is the most complete and nutritious in the world. Consumers have been reminded to disregard any suggestions that food supplements can be relied on as a treatment for any ailment requiring medical attention. Postmasters everywhere have been urging residents to report instances of medical fraud involving use of the mail.

Late in 1957 there was another plea for more practical nurses by Dr. Carl N. Neupert, State of Wisconsin Health Officer, who added to his great number of timely health contributions by making known the following:

> As our state population increases each year, the demand for nurses and other medical personnel also increases. Trained practical nurses are needed more than ever to help in filling the gap between the demand for nursing services and the available supply.
>
> The trained practical nurse is a person prepared by an accredited educational program to share in the care of patients requiring nursing services in institutions and at home. She works at all times under the direction of a licensed physician or a registered nurse.
>
> In the years before licensing, most practical nurses were employed for private practice in homes. Today a large

number serve in convalescent or nursing homes and in general hospitals.

Officials of the U. S. Public Health Service lately have been repeating that yellow fever, smallpox, and cholera are threatening to invade this country by way of ships and ports. These diseases have been steadily spreading through Asia, Africa, and Latin America. Another menace, the virus of influenza, already has swept through the Orient, the Philippine Islands, and the United States.

In an effort to set up effective-control measures in this country, the Public Health Service has been seeking enough funds from Congress to warrant employing 40 additional inspectors at international airports.

"With a continuous northward movement of yellow fever," Dr. Calvin Spencer warns, "there is great potential danger of its introduction in the United States via travel and commerce by way of surface vessels, planes, trains, and motor vehicles."

Luckily for us, smallpox no longer is a terror here. With reference to it, Dr. Spencer has stated that, for a third consecutive year, as a result of the tightest controls, our country has remained free of this disease. Epidemics have gone raging in South America, Asia, and Africa.

All persons, when arriving at a U. S. port of entry, both alien and citizen, are required to show evidence that they have been vaccinated against smallpox within the last three years. Any lowering of these standards in this country could easily lead to serious outbreaks.

Getting back to the topic of yellow fever, its germ is carried by mosquitoes, and it now has many ways of getting into the United States. It has been found as far north as Southern Texas, reports the Quarantine Division chief. It definitely is a menace in our Southern and Southeastern states, where receptive conditions for urban-yellow fever exist, principally in the form of the Aedes Aegypti mosquito and non-immune, human population.

Insects can reach this country not only on ships but by means of motor vehicles and the ever-increasing aircraft.

Through the continuous movement of travelers and

traffic, the virulent disease called yellow fever is being brought to our southern border steadily and easily.

Most astounding is a calculation made recently by a member of the American Medical Association in the field of psychosomatic. He said that three-fourths of the patients visiting their physicians today actually are suffering from ailments that are psychosomatic, rather than purely physical.

While these new problems are being faced, medical authorities are saying that, to maintain the current ratio of physicians to general population, an additional 25 schools are needed. A total of 82 now are conducting approved courses.

By 1977, approximately 750 million dollars will be required for capital investment in medical-education facilities. New wonder capsules and tablets, no doubt, will add much impetus to ethical-drug manufacturing during the next ten years. Surely the progress made in antibiotics during the last decade was tremendous. Currently our Food and Drug Administration is approving 300 new drugs a year. Companies manufacturing them now total 250. More than a billion dollars are being spent yearly in this country for prescriptions. Since the end of World War II, the increase has been nearly 200 percent.

Babies are being immunized with Salk vaccine as early as six weeks of age, reports Dr. Randolph Batson of Nashville, Tenn. A new synthetic drug, propoxyphene hydrochloride, is as effective in relieving pain as is codeine and it has some advantages, said Dr. Charles M. Gruber, Jr., of Indianapolis General Hospital, in comments published recently in the American Medical Society's Journal. This drug, said Gruber, was developed chiefly for the purpose of making our country independent of foreign-opium supplies from which codeine comes.

First-aid techniques, with changes based on new medical views, are described in a handbook published by the Red Cross. A hygienist again points out the health hazard created by a youngster in school who puts a pencil in the mouth and then loans it to another child who, too, has a habit of wetting the lead.

Danger from a puncture wound caused by a pencil, the hygienist warns, is that germs may be carried into tissues from the skin surface. A wound of this type is very narrow in width. It closes quickly, permitting blood and serum to clot. Germs are given an ideal growing place. Infection is encouraged, for the wound is difficult to clean.

As a helpful hint for grandma when she breaks a hip, Dr. Garrett Pipkin, orthopedic authority of Kansas City, says she probably should have a hot toddy while waiting for the ambulance.

As 1958 was under way, Grandma's health was endangered by new germs in the air, called Asian flu. Everyone in the world was faced with the same danger.

When this new and highly infectious form of influenza was sweeping through Japan, causing 190,000 children to become ill and 800 schools to close, the people of Wisconsin and elsewhere were informed that in short time the epidemic would be striking them hard. Soon it was learned that the virus had entered the bloodstreams of 250,000 persons at Hong Kong. Months later it was on its widespread course of destruction in this country, hitting 300,000 residents in 20 states, quickly spreading into the other population centers.

Louisiana was weakened by the new type of bug. Within a week, Mississippi alone had 20,000 cases. As health authorities everywhere were girding for battle, Wisconsinites were told that 22,600 doses of vaccine had been allocated to them.

At Houston, Texas, the postmaster said his 2,650 employees should be given the vaccine in order to avoid stoppage of the mail. The U. S. Surgeon General predicted that the rate of attack generally would be approximately 20%. By February 1, 1958, he said, the amount of vaccine dispensed to physicians at large would be 60,000,000 c.c. Another news release, issued by Dr. David D. Rutstein, head of the Harvard University Department of Preventive Medicine, made known a stockpiling of antibiotics as a defense against pneumonia germs—the hardest of complications in flu cases.

While danger signals were flying, a United Press survey showed 421 deaths caused by flu and its various complications during the summer of '57. Between September 1 and October 18, the Associated Press said, deaths in 108 cities had exceeded by 692 the number recorded during that same period the year before. At Mellen, Wis., schools were being closed. At Iron River, school absences reached an influenza high of 65%. At Ashland, a football game between the high schools of Ashland and Ironwood was cancelled when 275 Ironwood students were hard hit by the flu. In Texas, Southern Methodist University reported 200 cases overnight. Person-to-person contacts at Texas A & M College resulted in a quick spread there. Absences at Houston public schools, rising to 1,600 or more, revealed upper-respiratory infections alarming in scope.

By this time the U. S. Public Health Service said an additional 1,100,000 persons in 38 states had been stricken by various types of flu, raising the nation-wide total to nearly six million cases. In a single week throughout Wisconsin, the estimated number of cases was 86,682, one-fourth of which were in Milwaukee. Other communities reporting 1,000 or more cases at that time were Fond du Lac, Sheboygan, Eau Claire, Appleton, and Oshkosh.

Everywhere this epidemic was flaring up. At Washington, D. C., grid contests were cancelled. Across the continent in Salt Lake City, church meetings were postponed indefinitely. In a single week at El Paso, private physicians treated 752 flu-type infections. Then the U. S. Public Health Service announced that a new and more powerful vaccine was being released. Persons who had been vaccinated only once were urged to get a second shot. Another 50 deaths were reported by the Associated Press. From Oregon and California to Oklahoma, Colorado, Missouri, Indiana, Illinois, Michigan, Ohio, Pennsylvania, New Jersey, and New York, said the leased-wire reporters, new respiratory diseases were being confirmed.

At Madison, Wis., as many as 5,000 students were kept out of school in one day. President Eisenhower's radio talk stressed health and medical needs. In Puerto Rico, where the epidemic was at its peak, an additional 129,000 cases were fully taxing the doctors' physical resources. It was merely another reminder that Asian flu had spread around the world in 20 weeks. So widespread was its attack that, in Wisconsin late in '57, the State Health Officer said it had outdistanced the use of vaccine.

"In communities where the disease has reached epidemic proportions," he asserted, "it is too late in most cases to use the vaccine."

Never in all history before 1957 were stories concerning an epidemic so recurrent, so diligently read, so informative, so beneficial.

Interesting were statements made by Dr. F. M. Davenport, director of the Committee on Influenza of the Armed Forces Epidemiological Board, regarding immunity.

"Evidence," he said, "is increasing that older sections of the population have developed protective antibodies against disease, presumably from a long-ago exposure to the virus, or one like it. At first, it was believed, no one had immunity to the new strain. The elderly are less likely to get influenza than the young, but they run a greater risk of complications if infected."

In Colorado, more than 1,000 military men at Fort Carson were hit. At the University of Colorado, nearly 700 students were confined to the infirmary with that microscopic bug called Asian flu. Schools, industry, business, government, church organizations all had to become victims of their attacks.

History tells us that influenza is not a 20th century newcomer. During the Crusades it was a mankiller in Germany, England, and Italy. Of the four known flu pandemic in the last 175 years, the 1957-58 sweep was the least fatal.

Turning to a subject of pleasant interest, let's read what Carl N. Neupert, State of Wisconsin Health Officer, has to say concerning expectant parents:

> It is quite natural that expectant parents, although they may look forward to parenthood, wonder if they'll be good parents and what changes the new baby will make in their lives. Often the sharing of ideas and feelings with others who are facing the same experience is of real help.
>
> In many Wisconsin communities, expectant parents are attending group

meetings in order to learn and exchange ideas about parenthood. These expectant-parent classes are being held in 39 areas at the present time. Most of them are attended by mothers only, but they do include fathers for part of the course if both the mothers and fathers want to participate. Class leaders are usually public-health nurses. The classes are approved by local physicians, and hospitals and vocational schools are often cooperating or sponsoring agencies.

What goes on in expectant-parent classes?

Each group differs a bit, of course, but the goal of all classes is to provide an educational experience which will help prospective parents to build up confidence in their abilities and decisions. The common problems and expectations of these young parents form the core of the discussions carried on in expectant-parent meetings. Information on pregnancy, childbirth, and child development is interrelated with the meaning of the situations which are likely to arise in connection with parent-child relationships.

Ready-made answers are not provided in the classes. Instead, the prospective parents are free to take from the experience what they are able to use in their own individual cases.

Information about location of classes in any particular community can be obtained from the parents' physician, the county nurse, or city-health department.

Wisconsin's classes in parent education are one way of helping parents give their children the best possible chance to develop good physical and emotional health.

All of which is a reminder that the longest life is short, that we should make it count, and that we all should have full recognition of the importance of the body—that creation of God which houses our greatest possession—the soul. Recommended for reading are enlightening details concerning heart surgery on Page 490 of Encyclopedia Britannica's *1957 Book of the Year* edition, which also offers invaluable information regarding cancer, Parkinson's disease, and a newly-prevalent condition called *Pulseless* which is found in young women.

How tempus fugits!

Quick proof is in a review of Wisconsin's colorful past.

If Ethel Theodora Rockwell were to put on a medical pageant in the University of Wisconsin stadium, portraying all of the historical events since early territorial days, with Ray Dvorak's band furnishing the music for pompous actors, the drama would far exceed that of 1936 when the biggest stage ever built in Wisconsin and the largest number of actors ever assembled in a Grecian-like amphitheater here insured nation-wide centennial fame.

That event, it seems, was not so long ago; and the star performances of Frank L. "Hootie" Weston as an end for the University of Wisconsin football team seem to be in the immediate past. Yet several decades have elapsed since that year of 1920 when Weston, "Rowdy" Elliott, Guy Sundt, Gus Tebell, Rollie Williams, and Ralph Scott combined their gridiron skills to give Wisconsin one of its most powerful teams, with only one loss—that to Big 10 Champion Ohio State.

As an all-time Wisconsin football luminary, picked by Walter Eckersall for mythical All-Western honors prior to his graduation from the medical school, Doc Weston has been a bulwark of strength within the State Medical Society.

Currently a clinical professor of medicine, University Hospitals, steadfastly active in committee work for the state organization of doctors, long in the House of Delegates, an officer whose expertness in building a strong treasury was one of the key factors in modern Society successes, Dr. Weston symbolizes the spirit which, since 1841, has laid the foundation for Wisconsin's ever strengthening public health. Both he and Ivan B. Williamson, as members of the University of Wisconsin Athletic Board, are challenges to our youth.

Again, with thoughts in retrospect, there is great inspiration in that "In Memoriam" on Dr. Andrew J. Ward, published by the Military Order of the Loyal Legion of the United States in July, 1893, now recorded in our State Historical Society. It is as follows:

In Memoriam

Death has claimed one of our oldest and best known companions—one who gave much of his active life to his country. Brevet Lieutenant Colonel Andrew Jackson Ward, Surgeon, died at Hornellsville, New York, July 10th, 1893, and was buried at Madison, Wisconsin.

During war with Mexico, he enlisted in the 1st New York regiment, at Bath, New York, June, 1846, and was subsequently commissioned Assistant Surgeon. Serving with his regiment in California, he was stationed at various posts as medical officer. From this service, he was honorably discharged in September, 1848. Some years later he moved to Wisconsin with his family.

When the War of the Rebellion opened, Companion Ward promptly tendered his services, and was commissioned Surgeon of the second regiment Wisconsin Infantry. No medical officer in the Union Army was more efficient and indefatigable in the discharge of every duty—kind and considerate to all who were under his charge, enthusiastic in his efforts to do all that was possible for their comfort—never neglecting any one, high or low—as attentive to the private soldier as he was to the highest in rank. Genial, affectionate and untiring, he won, and deserved, the love and esteem of all of his comrades.

His record in the Army of the Potomac was highly honorable. He was often sought for by his superiors to act as Brigade and Division Surgeon and was at times in charge of Division and Corps hospitals. Wherever he was placed on duty, he did not fail to win the praises of his superiors and the gratitude of the wounded and sick under his care. For especially efficient service in that Army, he was commissioned Brevet Lieutenant Colonel by the President of the United States.

Within two months after his honorable discharge from the 2nd Wisconsin in 1864, Companion Ward again mustered into the service as Surgeon of the 43d regiment Wisconsin Infantry. With that regiment, he gave the same considerate and efficient attention to every duty that fell to his lot to discharge, and continued to enjoy the confidence of his comrades of every rank. For a time he served on the staff of General Thomas.

Nor did Surgeon Ward cease his attention to the necessities of his comrades when the war was over. During the many years since our armies were laid aside, he was ever active in striving to be of service to them. No one of them ever called upon him in vain. Such professional or personal attention as he could give to them was never refused whether the comrade was rich or poor—with him it was a labor of love. Thousands of our comrades remember him with loving affection. A loyal, brave citizen and affectionate friend has gone to join his comrades beyond the grave."

(signed)   LUCIUS FAIRCHILD,
    Brig. General, U.S.V.

WILLIAM P. LYON,
    Col., 13th Wis. Inf.,
    Brevet Brig. Gen., U.S.V.

M. J. CANTWELL,
    1st Lieut., 12th Wis. Inf.,
    U.S.V.
                            Committee.

A fitting tribute for a doctor who, as old comrades said in their written testimonial, had regarded his daily work as a labor of love in both war and peace.

At death, Dr. Ward was 69, two decades beyond that age when the average citizen was cut down by injury or disease. He didn't live to see the advent of wonder drugs and miraculous surgery.

At 19, in 1843, he was in a medical-lecture course at the University of Pennsylvania and had completed three semesters of study by the time he enlisted for war service against Mexico.

Dr. Ward's medical practice at Madison began in 1850.

While the first regiments were on their way to battlesites at the start of the War Between the States in '61, he was appointed temporarily to the position of surgeon.

Soon thereafter, following the Battle of Bull Run, 37-year-old Ward was commissioned surgeon of the 2n Wisconsin Infantry, Iron Brigade.

Imagine the year-in-and-year-out ordeals he had to live through while giving medical service to men wounded at Antietam, Fredericksburg, Fitzhugh's Crossing, Chancellorsville, and Gettysburg.

Casualties were enormous.

At Antietam, where as many as 2,000 men of the Northern Army were killed in a single hour, death took a total of 12,000.

At Chancellorsville, midway between Washington and Richmond, wounds were vast in number and the death toll list was long in what was one of the decisive battles of the war.

At Gettysburg, best known for Lincoln's immortal speech, regarded by reliable historians as the turning point of that holocaust, one particular Northern regiment alone lost 90 per cent of its men. General Meade's fighting forces there were cut from 82,000 to approximately 59,000. Southern General Lee's losses in killed, wounded and missing totaled 30,000.

Imagine the vastness of the agony on those battlefields, with anaesthesia scarce and often unobtainable—no chloroform or ether, no antiseptic surgery for men whose bleeding wounds were causing unbearable pain, made worse by the surgeon's repair action with knife, hands, and needle, within hearing distance of thundering cannons and the surgeon's efficiency not of the best as the result of fatigue, undernourishment, disappointment, and shock.

Every surgeon on every field of battle then was a victim of cruel reality, especially when working on a torn stomach, chest, face, or spine, without the knowledge and the skill possessed by 20th century surgeons, yet giving the best possible service on a basis of the established standards of that time, when college training was best known for what it was unable to offer.

Butchery it was—honorable, dignified, human butchery, made necessary by the fact that as many lives as possible had to be saved, no matter how awful the pain during an nonanaesthetic, emergency operation which was shrouded in tense uncertainties for both surgeon and wounded men.

Experiments were on a basis of whatever techniques the weary doctor was able to develop hastily in his own way, without antisepsis and other aids from science, some experiments proving successful, others an unpreventable failure as a conscious patient fought pain and did his best to keep his heart from collapsing.

Because of no advanced knowledge of asepsis and antisepsis in the treatment of fractures, the practice of amputation was common. Surgeons considered it a duty.

What patience! What tolerance! What pressure on one's nervous system! What reliability and what valour from one terrifying battle to another for many years! What endurance! What physical and mental strength!

What objectives and what faith in country, its aims, and its ideals as each zealous army surgeon kept working through the agonies of wounded men undergoing surgery without anaesthesia, or dying on field of battle, shrieking and groaning, without any medical aid!

What courage as a surgeon's saw was cutting away an arm or a leg!

Only the strongest of the great, with God's help, could emerge successfully from such horridness, and Madison's Doctor Ward was one of them. Not only that, according to honored men of his regiment who survived with him, his service truly had been a labor of love in spite of the vastness of the tragedies he had experienced.

Of equally great importance, Ward's post-war outlook was of the best, unchanged by time and events, as proven by his kindness, warmth of fellowship, and gratefulness, which he never lost.

Another survivor of distinction was Phillip Fox, whose first job was on a farm and his first formalized schooling at Sinsinawa.

A graduate of Bellevue Hospital College in New York City, Fox served as an assistant surgeon with the 2nd Regiment, Wisconsin Volunteer Infantry; and at the time of his death, he had practiced medicine in Madison for 36 years.

Contributions by other medical doctors to worthy-community enterprises in the past have been of such general scope that a detailed account of it all would fill many volumes of printer's type; and one biographical sketch on Dr. Joseph Hobbins of Madison, immediately after his death in January, 1894, written by Reuben Gold Thwaites, superior historian and researcher when serving as State Historical Society head, is reprinted in part herewith as follows:

> Dr. Hobbins had led a quiet, professional career, but it was in many ways eminently useful to his state and city; and it might, in its active enjoyment and promotion of the best things in life, rightfully be called ideal.

The State University was in its early formative stage when Dr. Hobbins came to Madison, and its regiments had just determined to open a medical department. Chancellor Lathrop intrusted our friend with the task of organizing the school, appointing him professor of surgery; but the University in those days was suffering from official neglect and mismanagement. So the project fell through.

Later, when a member of the Common Council, the Doctor was efficient in organizing a local Board of Health. He made a strong stand for a city hospital. When the War of Secession broke out, Dr. Hobbins organized the medical corps at Camp Randall, where he also was surgeon in charge of the sick Confederate prisoners sent here from the South.

The Doctor was not a one-sided man. He dearly loved his profession, and stood stoutly for its old-time code of ethics. Too, he had a keen appreciation for the best in art and literature and was a practical horticulturalist. As first secretary of the Madison Horticultural Society, he was for 12 years the president. For five years he was president of the State Society. Old Madison residents remember his annual exhibition of flowers and fruit. He encouraged the planting of trees and shrubbery.

The last years of Dr. Hobbins' life were chiefly given to the Madison Literary Club, which he founded in 1877; was president up to the time of his death.

We have seen that Dr. Hobbins was prominent in his profession, a pioneer in horticulture, a promoter of literary activity, and in every beneficient public enterprise, a leading spirit. He was even more than this—he was a man of noble aspirations, his nature was pure, his human sympathies warm, his judgment sound. So it followed that his influence in this community was always for the best.

Inspiring in retrospect is this tribute, paid by the greatest Wisconsin historian of that day to a 19th century doctor of high repute. It represents a lifetime of distinguished public service.

Records of progress in Wisconsin were used as the basis for Dr. Gunnar Gundersen's presidential address to the House of Delegates in 1941.

Showing his planned foresight concerning a centennial section in the Society's Blue Book, Gundersen said:

> This outline of the first century of progress is the first step in the direction of developing a current section devoted to the public health and medical economic work of the profession. It was largely inspired as a result of the interest shown during the Society's centennial meeting, when the historical survey of medicine in Wisconsin proved a fascinating topic for members of our profession.

In this address at centennial time, the very distinguished LaCrosse doctor pointed out the medical logic expressed in 1871 by the Society's thirteenth president—H. B. Strong of Beloit. Quoting Strong, he said:

> Medicine is, at present, in the midst of one of these transitions. I'd have you act honestly and intelligently. The danger in a transition period lies in the tendency of the human mind to oscillate to extremes. The great problem at such times should be the fusion or amalgamation of the great elements of all existence, stability and progress — the great desideratum, fidelity to our inheritances from

the past, and a cordial welcome to the invitations of the future.

Dr. Gundersen then declared:

> So what could be more appropriate at this period of our growth than to rededicate ourselves and our Society to the proposition of a life of service to our fellow citizens, and during the century ahead, join with our state under its banner and slogan 'Forward.'

When this address was given by Dr. Gundersen, devastating epidemics were of the dim past. Diphtheria and typhoid fever no longer were imperiling the public health. State-wide controls were of the best, with only one death caused by typhoid fever in 1942, compared with 558 in 1910, when 2,446 persons were stricken. As for the triumph by science over diphtheria, it is best proven by the state record of '42, when five diphtheria patients failed to avoid the grave. In 1910, peak year of epidemics, death took 429 diphtheria patients.

In evaluating these conditions of the past, one has a huge appreciation for the great health and medical improvements that have been realized during the last decade, as shown in the personal touch of Dr. L. O. Simenstad to the scientific excellence of our present-day, medical profession, taken from the President's Page of the Wisconsin Medical Journal, dated November 1956. It is as follows:

> During the past few months, I have had the opportunity to attend meetings of physicians in many parts of the state. During a break in a meeting at Lancaster, Doctor Howell of Fennimore suggested that I accompany him to see his patients in the Lancaster Memorial Hospital. I was amazed. Here in a small community was a well-equipped hospital with fine x-ray facilities, operating, delivery, and patient rooms, all spotlessly clean and restful. This hospital and its staff is rendering excellent service to the

people of Lancaster. It was told that Boscobel and Platteville have similar new hospitals.

I began to think of the many fine new hospitals in Wisconsin, including the one here in Osceola. Public-spirited citizens, with some federal help at times, and with the cooperation of the State Board of Health and Mr. Vincent Otis, Director of the Board's Division of Hospital and Related Services, have certainly improved the medical care in rural communities. And once the facilities are there, no one would give them up.

I thought, too, of the many advances in medicine—things that have made people live longer and more happily such as penicillin, insulin, Salk vaccine for polio, delicate heart surgery, and many other technical procedures.

Then I began to wonder further. With all this fine progress in medical care, have we kept the 'art of practice' in tune with the times? It is not alone because of our own efforts that we are in an honored profession. Physicians are revered in part because the older family doctors and those who have gone before us, whether they knew it or not, had good patient relations. They, like present practitioners, were honest in their attempts to help patients, but they had one unusual trait—they had to make up in personal intent what they lacked in knowledge.

We have a great heritage. The members of our profession are highly honorable men. Let's not allow a few physicians to make it appear that doctors are selfish, unsympathetic, and interested only in their personal gain. Each of us, by adding the personal touch to his scientific excellence, can help keep the medical profession in its high place of public esteem, concluded Dr. Simenstad.

The history of medicine, as defined by Oliver Wendell Holmes, immortal New England writer and physician, is most enlightening. It is as follows:

> Medicine learned from a monk how to use antimony, from a Jesuit how to cure agues, from a friar how to cut for stone, from a soldier how to treat gout, from a sailor how to keep off scurvy, from a postmaster how to sound the Eustachian tube, from a dairymaid how to prevent smallpox, and from an old market woman how to catch the itch-insect.

Holmes, born during James Madison's first year as president, a half century before Pasteur's discovery of germs, was one of those fortunate persons whose appendix didn't sentence him to death. His span of life was prior to painless surgery and miracle drugs. Fortunately for him, during his many decades as a writer, editor, and professor, milk-borne diseases didn't enter his bloodstream.

Unknown then was pasteurization — that wonderful control over the dangerous organisms originating in the cow. Government dairy regulations were unheard of; and without any standards of cleanliness anywhere, milk often became contaminated while in distribution.

In closing this testimonial to all grand knights of medicine of past and present throughout our Badger State, your very humble historian quotes Malcolm W. Bingay, scholarly Detroit writer, as follows:

> Remember the doctor who fought his way through the snowdrifts and the sleet for hours to reach an isolated home by daybreak?
>
> There was no thought of financial reward from that destitute family. A knight in the armor of his profession just was living up to the oath of Hippocrates.
>
> Thus it is that, in every hour of life, the Good Doctor shakes dice with destiny.

He sees life from the first feeble cry to the last sigh, and though oft he shields himself with a protecting crust of cynicism, deep down in his heart he walks humbly with God.

Oh, the glory of the years that lie behind and the promise of the vista that stretches forth to the future!

Out of the terrors of darkness and superstition the men of medicine are guiding groping mankind.

War, with all its bloody history of brave deeds, cannot match the sublime courage of the valiant host in white whose names are forever emblazoned on the honor rolls of the healing art.

The plagues that once swept the world have been largely eliminated. Every generation shows that their conquerors have given to mankind a longer span of life. Man is healthier and happier, because of the mighty legionnaires of medicine.

So, to you, the Guardians of Life, know thee this — that your profession is on the threshold of vast new discoveries that will revolutionize life on this earth. For you alone remains the romance of great adventure.

In this new, strangely complicated civilization into which we are rushing today, to you is dedicated the great task of not only keeping man alive but, more: keeping man's faith in himself.

No man, no profession, has any higher call to duty: "For of the most High cometh healing."

To these hallowed words from Malcolm Bingay's feature article, we pay prayerful tribute to every worthy Wisconsin doctor of past and present. We'd like to see a *Hall of True Eminence* built at Fort Crawford in their honor, with names inscribed on panels that cannot be affected by time, temperature, fire, or storm.

Truly the story of medicine in Wisconsin assumes its proper place in the ever-expanding narrative covering medical development on this continent. It is an integral part of the story of our nation. It reflects the factors which were evident throughout this country in corresponding periods. It definitely is an integral segment of world history.

All of which is a reminder that, to foresee our future intelligently, we first must be cognizant of our knowledge concerning our past; and in this broad field of medicine, relating to health, mortality rate, and other interlocking factors which, in reality, serve as a barometer for our nation's vitality and progress, it should be the duty of every civic leader, every historian, every educator, and all others who are interested in life's better objectives, including men of government, to take an active part in this project sponsored by the State Medical Society of Wisconsin in acquiring all funds needed for the physical completion of its shrine at Prairie du Chien. Gifts should flow like Copper Falls.

To help promote educational needs, public leaders everywhere should work in harness to get this work completed. To help future generations develop a full recognition of the miraculous medical discoveries achieved for them, let's make that needed contribution which now is a challenge for us! Let's prove the extent of our faith in things uplifting and beneficial!

How lucky we are, living in an era hundreds of years beyond that of the Spaniards who, when coming to this continent after Columbus, were unable to bring any practical or advanced medical knowledge with them, were eager to learn herb-therapy from Indians whose instincts and crude experiments had been their only medical guides, along with deception and superstition.

Not until early years of the nineteenth century, in fact, did any records on this continent begin to reveal much concerning disease, doctors, or hospitals.

How fortunate we are in not having lived among those people of the wilderness who, as victims of the scourge called smallpox, were in a most horrible struggle against death, their lifeless bodies falling to the ground in pieces when removed from their tents.

How dreadful it must have been in 1874, prior to antisepsis, when yellow fever was rampant in certain parts of our continent, with valiant doctors striving to control it by way of calomel, quinine, Dover's powders, and brandy.

Now, with heads bowed and eyes closed, let's tell God in prayer how thankful we are for His goodness in giving strength and grace to those men of medicine in the dim past who, isolated from knowledge that was yet to come, were truly great, developing a versatility and an independence which we must admire and recapture.

THE HONOR ROLL

J. G. CROWNHART

In starting to take you through this department called *Honor Roll*, it is fitting to first remember the great leadership furnished throughout the fore part of this century by J. "George" Crownhart, who, as secretary of the State Medical Society, led key officers to the upper rungs of the achievement ladder. Fighting epidemics the year 'round was the Society's biggest problem in those decades. Doctor John Morris Dodd, fighter extraordinary, often said that "George" Crownhart's services were indispensable.

C. H. CROWNHART

In harness as secretary of the State Medical Society since January, 1942, following in the service of his brother, the indefatigable C. H. Crownhart has earned for himself a niche in the Society's realm of eminence. An ever increasing membership, widely expanding committee projects, strengthened House of Delegates, bigger and better annual meetings, the construction of a museum at Prairie du Chien, and the restoration of the military hospital at Old Fort Crawford all reflect his administrative successes.

THE JACKSON FAMILY IN RETROSPECT

Most endearing is that record of eminence left by James Albert Jackson, Madison drug clerk, who, as an assistant surgeon with Wisconsin's Eagle Regiment throughout the Civil War, was capable of facing grim reality with unwavering faith, striving to save lives on fields of battle, where the rate of slaughter was ghastly high and unsanitary conditions developing into devastating epidemics, with pneumonia quickly following in the wake of measles, vastly reducing the military strength through suffering and death.

After Appomattox, James Albert Jackson was cogently determined to give his country his best civilian service among the sick, as shown in his studies at Bellevue Medical College and his long career as a physician-surgeon at Madison, that great city of art, education, government, science, religion, industry, letters, and medicine, where a clinic of national repute bears Jackson's name.

On the honor roll with him are three sons as follows:

Reginald H. Jackson, graduate of Columbia University School of Medicine, widely known for his internal-surgery successes, a professor of surgery at the University of Wisconsin School of Medicine, a past president of State Medical Society, for decades one of Dane County's aggressive public-health crusaders.

James A. Jackson, Jr., brother of Reginald and Arnold, a scholar of the highest rank while in training for the medical profession, a specialist in surgery, long the Milwaukee Railroad Company's chief surgeon, active in county, state, and national medical associations, in practice with his brothers at Jackson Clinic.

Arnold S. Jackson, a graduate of Wisconsin and Columbia Universities, with a Mayo Foundation fellowship in surgery and a Mayo degree of M.S., active in Medical Society projects, known nationally as a goiter surgeon.

Now a big salute goes to the Twohig combination of brothers at Fond du Lac—namely, H. E., J. E., and Dave, closely knit brothers who set up one of Wisconsin's best clinics soon after graduation from medical school. Family greatness in our medical profession is a trademark of the Quislings at Madison; father-and-son combinations are many, and such names as Tenney, Wilkinson, Helm, Smiles, Davis, Hoyer, Burke, Vedder, Prentice, Fox, Gundersen, Hipke, Dodd, Shearer, Bachhuber, Franklin, Tasche, and Harrison all tend to be colorful in retrospect.

The present George W. Harrison at Ashland is the grandson of that backwoods physician-surgeon who in the late 1880s rode on the back of a horse between Ashland and Cable regularly in snowstorms and rain to give service to logging-camp employes. His father, practicing long before the era of wonder drugs and miracle surgery, carried on the traditions of his pioneering parent for many decades. All are saluted here.

An honor roll without J. W. Kleinboehl of Milwaukee on it would be the same as a baseball team which starts a game with only eight players.

A famous German surgeon, specializing in urology and gynecology, recognized by the Marquette faculty as a diagnostician of national repute, popularly referred to as the family physician of Joseph Uhlein and Fred Pabst, with nearly 100 reference doctors between Chicago and Milwaukee, J. W. Kleinboehl tried to retire three different times as old age was setting in, but each time his army of boosters forced him to change his mind.

The list of distinguished Wisconsin doctors, once completed, would be panoramic in itself. It would include Wm. D. Stovall of Madison, long of the State Society's House of Delegates, whose most recent achievement as a builder is shown in his activity as chairman of the Medical History committee, insuring the restoration of Fort Crawford Military Hospital as a museum. A past State Society president, Stovall exemplifies that spirit which for many decades has made Wisconsin a leader in gainful health-improvement projects.

At this point we'll honor the Marquette School of Medicine, whose current dean, John S. Hirschboeck, in harness there since 1947, has been a key speaker and committeeman in State Medical Society. As dean now at Marquette, Dr. Hirschboeck is the fourth in line of service, following Eben J. Carey, Bernard F. McGrath, and Louis Jermain. The latter was at the helm in 1913, when a merger of the Milwaukee Medical College and the Wisconsin College of Physicians and Surgeons resulted in the establishment of Marquette. Since that time, endowments of more than $2,000,000 have given the Marquette authorities an opportunity to set up museums of national fame, one containing more than 4,000 specimens of gross pathology, a library of 10,000 or more slides of pathological histology and bacteria, et cetera, the other museum containing anatomical subjects vast in scope.

In Madison we salute W. S. Middleton, dean of the Wisconsin Medical School; we are mindful of what Erastus B. Wolcott did for sick people who were under his care; we continue to see A. A. Pleyte of Milwaukee waging the most effective fight against tuberculosis; we are cognizant that, of all the great surgeons, W. J. Tucker of Ashland is worthy of wide homage; and in that same city on Chequamegon Bay is a new clinic which stands out as a monument to middle twentieth-century progress, built by Harry H. and Jeri D. Larson.

Because of the overwhelming aspects of research, this honor roll is incomplete. If the name of your favorite doctor is not found in this book, feel assured that he or she is not forgotten in the annals of medical history. It is easy for anyone to make an insertion anywhere in this section of the book.

Immortal in our field of psychiatry is Dr. William Lorenz, long a University of Wisconsin professor, a U. S. Public Health Service consultant, popularly called "Wisconsin's pioneer in psychiatry," a veteran of Spanish-American War and World War I, graduate of New York University, one of the first doctors in our nation to study the oxygen metabolism of the brain, director of the Wisconsin Psychiatric Institute, chairman of the old State Board of Control, long active in legislation to provide better hospitalization for the mentally ill, well known in the medical profession of countries abroad, who, with Dr. A. S. Loevenhart, produced tryparsamine, the first useful drug in the treatment of syphilis of the nervous system, and who for a long period was chairman of the Wisconsin athletic board.

A CAVALCADE OF STATE LEADERSHIP

Now saluting the State Medical Society presidents, who, since 1847, have served in the following order:

Mason C. Darling, Fond du Lac; J. B. Dousman, Milwaukee; A. L. Castleman, Delafield; Harmon Van Dusen, Mineral Point; John Mitchell, Janesville; D. Cooper Ayres, Green Bay; Clark G. Pease, Janesville; E. S. Carr, Madison; Solomon Blood, Rochester; Solon Marks, Milwaukee; H. P. Strong, Beloit; John Favill, Madison; M. Waterhouse, Portage; J. T. Reeve, Appleton; J. B. Whiting, Janesville; J. K. Bartlett, Milwaukee; Darius Mason, Prairie du Chien; Nicholas Senn, Milwaukee; J. G. Meacher, Portage; T. P. Russell, Oshkosh; N. M. Dobson, Berlin; E. W. Bartlett, Milwaukee; G. M. Steele, Oshkosh; S. C. Johnson, Hudson; L. G. Armstrong, Boscobel; J. R. Barnett, Neenah; E. M. Rogers, Hartford; G. D. Ladd, Milwaukee; G. F. Witter, Grand Rapids; B. T. Phillips, Menominee, Mich.; B. C. Brett, Green Bay; Almon Clarke, Sheboygan; F. W. Epley, New Richmond; B. O. Reynolds, Lake Geneva;

William Mackie, Milwaukee; Herman Reineking, Milwaukee; W. T. Sarles, Sparta; J. F. Pritchard, Manitowoc; W. H. Neilson, Milwaukee; J. V. R. Lyman, Eau Claire; F. E. Walbridge, Milwaukee; C. W. Oviatt, Oshkosh; J. R. Currens, Two Rivers; L. H. Pelton, Waupaca; W. E. Ground, Superior; Gilbert E. Seaman, Madison; Edward Evans, La Crosse; Byron M. Caples, Waukesha; John M. Dodd, Sr., Ashland; Arthur J. Patek, Milwaukee; Charles S. Sheldon, Madison; T. J. Redelings, San Diego; L. J. Jermain, Milwaukee; Hoyt E. Dearholt, Milwaukee; Gustave Windesheim, Kenosha; D. J. Hayes, Milwaukee; C. R. Bardeen, Madison; M. A. McGarty, La Crosse; S. Hall, Ripon; F. G. Connell, Oshkosh; Rock Sleyster, Wauwautosa; Wilson Cunningham, Platteville; Joseph F. Smith, Wausau; Arthur W. Rogers, Oconomowoc; John J. McGovern, Milwaukee;

Karl W. Doege, Marshfield; F. J. Gaenslen, Milwaukee; Cornelius A. Harper, Madison; Otho Fiedler, Sheboygan; Reginald H. Jackson, Madison; Stanley J. Seeger, Milwaukee; T. J. O'Leary, Superior; R. M. Carter, Green Bay; Stephen E. Gavin, Fond du Lac; James C. Sargent, Milwaukee; A. E. Rector, Appleton; R. G. Arveson, Frederic; R. P. Sproule, Milwaukee; Gunnar Gundersen, La Crosse; R. M. Kurten, Racine; Charles Fidler, Milwaukee; W. D. Stovall, Madison; A. H. Heidner, West Bend; J. C. Griffith, Milwaukee; H. Kent Tenney, Madison; Arthur J. McCarey, Green Bay; Ervin L. Bernhart, Milwaukee; F. E. Butler, Menomonie; P. R. Minahan, Green Bay; H. H. Christofferson, Colby; J. W. Truitt, Milwaukee; L. O. Simenstad, Osceola; and H. E. Kasten, Beloit, the latter assuming the presidency in May, 1957.

Now saluting one of the greatest Councils in State Society history, headed by Frederic's Doctor Arveson: W. D. James, Oconomowoc; L. H. Lokvam, Kenosha; N. A. Hill, Madison; J. H. Houghton, Wisconsin Dells; E. M. Dessloch, Prairie du Chien; A. H. Heidner, West Bend; G. W. Carlson, Appleton; J. C. Fox, La Crosse; J. M. Bell, Marinette; R. E. Garrison, Wisconsin Rapids; V. E. Ekblad, Superior; J. D. Leahy, Park Falls; and R. E. Galasinski, E. L. Bernhart, N. J. Wegmann, J. P. Conway, J. E. Conley, all of Milwaukee.

Now back to early territorial days to honor that little group of wilderness doctors who were empowered by law to form the parent Medical Society—namely, Bushnell B. Cary, Lucius I. Barber, Oliver E. Strong, Edward McSherry, E. W. Wolcott, J. C. Mills, David Walker, Horace White, Jonas P. Russell, David Ward, Jesse S. Hewett, B. O. Miller, and Mason C. Darling.

ASHLAND:

John M. Dodd, Sr.
W. E. Bargholtz
Edwin Ellis
J. E. Kreher
W. J. Tucker
J. M. Jauquet
C. J. Smiles
C. A. Grand
J. W. Prentice
Frank D. Weeks
A. H. Lamal
R. O. Grigsby
Will G. Merrill
K. A. Seifert
Albert Butler
The G. W. Harrisons
C. O. Hertzman
J. V. Wenzel
A. P. and Dell Andrus
John M. Dodd, Jr.
Adolph X. Kamm
M. W. Meyer
Wm. J. Smiles
W. T. Rinehart
H. V. Sandin
A. O. Shaw
Harry H. Larson
Jeri D. Larson
Braun
O'Brien
B. Culver Prentice

ANTIGO:

M. J. Donohue
B. W. Kromer
J. E. Garritty
W. P. Curran
E. G. Bloor
E. F. Dorzeski
M. A. Flatley
J. W. Lambert
E. A. McKenna
G. E. Moore
C. E. Zellmer

APPLETON:

W. O. Dehne
A. C. Taylor
C. D. Neidhold
H. T. Gross
W. E. Archer
J. L. Benton
E. L. Bolton
E. H. Brooks
W. J. Frawley
G. W. Carlson
D. M. Gallaher
W. S. Giffin
A. J. Gloss
W. J. Harrington
G. T. Hegner
F. J. Huberty
S. A. Konz
E. N. Krueger
J. W. Laird
R. V. Landis
J. B. MacLaren
V. F. Marshall
W. S. Marshall
L. B. McBain
R. T. McCarty
E. F. McGrath
E. F. Mielke
C. D. Neidhold
F. N. Pansch
C. A. Pardee
F. J. Rankin
A. E. Rector
J. S. Reeve
G. A. Ritchie
M. E. Swanton
A. C. Taylor
J. J. Young
E. J. Zeiss

BARABOO:

Roger Cahoon
A. C. Edwards
H. J. Irwin
Melvin F. Huth
J. F. Moon
C. R. Pearson
C. B. Pope
F. E. Tryon
H. Vander Kamp
F. R. Winslow

BEAVER DAM:

R. I. Bender
Xavier Corso
W. H. Costello
A. W. Hammond
A. G. Hough
A. A. Hoyer
E. C. Hoyer
G. H. Hoyer
R. R. Roberts
A. Rosenheimer
R. E. Schoen
R. F. Schoen
M. M. Temkin
E. P. Webb
J. M. Welsch

BELOIT:

V. D. Crone
H. A. Shearer
H. M. Helm
J. P. Allen
W. J. Allen
F. Brinckerhoff
E. B. Brown
H. E. Burger
C. M. Carney
W. W. Crockett
T. H. Flarity
B. Fosse
L. J. Friend
O. W. Friske
R. Gunderson
G. W. John
H. E. Kasten
J. W. Keithley
H. Kishpaugh
W. Mauermann
A. F. Ottow
H. A. Raube
M. E. Ross
H. Shearer
C. E. Smith
J. Springberg
R. A. Thayer
R. S. Vivian
R. F. Wilson

CHIPPEWA FALLS:

F. T. McHugh
W. C. Henske
C. Hatleberg
F. P. Daly
Merton Field
H. R. Hunter
J. A. Kelly
E. O. McCarty
F. T. McHugh
L. Patrick
L. W. Picotte
R. S. Rodgers
F. B. Sazama
A. J. Somers
S. E. Williams

EAU CLAIRE:

R. C. Frank
D. M. Willison

A. W. Hilker
A. A. Lorenz
S. B. Russell
W. R. Manz
K. E. Walter
F. G. Anderson
K. W. Baker
G. W. Beebe
R. A. Buckley
F. S. Cook
L. G. Culver
H. F. Derge
C. H. Falstad
H. S. Fuson
A. F. Haag
E. P. Hayes
S. L. Henke
A. J. Hertzog
G. Hoyme
H. C. Huston
C. M. Ihle
Fred Johnson
C. K. Kincaid
F. C. Kinsman
Martha Kohl
F. A. LaBreck
Lois Lobb
J. W. Lowe
E. L. Mason
W. T. Mautz
C. Midelfart
P. Midelfart
Mancel Mitchell
E. O. Niver
W. Paulson
P. Spelbring
H. M. Stang
R. C. Strand
J. W. Tanner
K. E. Walter
Nels Werner
R. F. Werner
J. H. Wishart
J. E. Ziegler

FOND DU LAC:

Stephen E. Gavin
W. H. Folsom
J. W. Wier
F. J. Cerny
D. W. McCormick
E. H. Pawsat
H. J. McLane
K. K. Borsack
D. W. Calvy
P. J. Clark
R. Dalrymple
R. L. Dana
H. A. Devine
W. C. Finn
A. C. Florin
L. C. Garnder
J. S. Huebner
A. M. Hutter
L. J. Keenan
H. J. Kief
O. M. Layton
C. W. Leonard
Howard Mauthe
P. G. McCabe
D. Meiklejohn
Nicholas Senn
H. R. Sharpe
L. J. Simon
E. V. Smith
E. V. Smith, Jr.
S. A. Theisen
P. J. Trier
Dave J. Twohig
D. J. Twohig, Jr.
H. E. Twohig
J. E. Twohig
W. Waldschmidt
D. N. Walters
F. S. Wiley
J. C. Yockey

GREEN BAY:

W. E. Leaper
A. J. McCarey
Charles Wunsch
George Nadeau
J. W. Nellen
Louis Milson
Frank Urben
Mary Allen
H. S. Atkinson
W. H. Bartran
A. H. Brusky
R. C. Buchanan
T. S. Burdon
Robert Burns
C. J. Chloupek
P. M. Clifford
J. C. Colignon
W. C. Comee
R. L. Cowles
F. L. Crikelair
G. F. Denys
K. J. Denys
P. F. Dockry
A. J. Dupont
A. A. Filak
J. L. Ford
W. W. Ford
M. H. Fuller
D. F. Gosin
M. A. Grossman
W. T. Hagerty
J. E. Halloin
H. H. Heitzman
H. Hendrickson
E. M. Jordan
W. A. Killins
R. W. Kispert
F. O. Kuhl
W. E. Leaper
I. E. Levitas
E. S. McNevins
P. R. Minahan
J. T. Murphy
E. J. O'Brien
A. O. Olmsted
L. D. Quigley
J. J. Robb
O. W. Saunders
E. S. Schmidt
George Senn
G. M. Shinners
G. R. Stauff
O. A. Stiennon
W. P. Tippet
R. L. Troup
W. J. Troup
C. S. Williamson

JANESVILLE:

H. C. Danforth
O. V. Overton
Francis Frechette
E. S. Hartlaub
G. W. Bartels
M. Baumgartner
F. C. Binnewies
W. T. Clark
M. A. Cunningham
F. B. Farnsworth
S. A. Freitag
C. R. Gilbertsen
E. C. Hartman
R. C. Hartman
M. E. Hatfield
W. L. Johnson
J. F. Kelley
T. W. Klein
V. W. Koch
F. H. Kuegle
G. S. Metcalf
W. A. Munn
T. O. Nuzum
T. W. Nuzum
O. V. Overton
A. H. Pember

T. J. Snodgrass
G. L. Thomas
F. W. VanKirk
G. C. Waufle
F. B. Welch

KENOSHA:

L. H. Lokvam
D. N. Goldstein
E. E. Bertolaet
J. T. Garren
Helen A. Binnie
E. F. Andre
T. W. Ashley
I. E. Bowing
J. H. Cleary
C. M. Creswell
F. D. Curtiss
C. C. Davin
S. F. DeFazio
C. H. Gephart
J. P. Graves
P. S. Herzog
B. S. Hill
P. P. Jorgensen
L. T. Kent
W. C. Kleinpell
W. H. Lipman
A. L. Mayfield
S. W. Murphy
C. E. Pechous
C. H. Perkins
P. E. Pifer
M. V. Pirsch
A. J. Randall
A. M. Rauch
L. M. Rauen
C. G. Richards
A. F. Ruffolo
A. Schlapik
G. C. Schulte
G. J. Schwartz
H. L. Schwartz
Theodore Sokow
W. C. Stewart
E. F. Swarthout
C. F. Ulrich
G. Windesheim

LA CROSSE:

J. C. Fox
J. E. Heraty
A. A. Solberg
G. B. Ridout
G. I. Uhrich
F. H. Wolfe
R. L. Gilbert
T. E. Gundersen
A. A. Cook
J. L. Jaeck
N. P. Anderson
W. E. Bannen
W. E. Bayley
E. S. Carlsson
D. M. Daley
F. A. Douglas
R. L. Eagan
G. J. Egan
L. W. Eidam
R. E. Flynn
E. E. Gallagher
F. L. Gallagher
S. Garrett-Bangsberg
P. C. Gatterdam
R. H. Gray
A. H. Gundersen
Gunnar Gundersen
S. B. Gundersen
T. E. Gundersen
J. C. Harman
Mary P. Houck
Russell Johnston
W. J. Jones
G. W. Lueck
M. A. McGarty

J. E. McLoone
S. A. Montgomery
C. J. Moran
G. R. Reay
W. H. Remer
J. A. Rosholt
J. A. Roth
E. J. Schneeberger
E. E. Seedorf
J. J. Simones
M. Siverton
A. A. Skemp
G. E. Skemp
D. S. Smith
Edyth C. Swarthout
E. H. Townsend
P. T. Walters
F. H. Wolf
H. E. Wolf

MADISON:

Frank L. Weston
N. A. Hill
Wm. D. Stovall
R. S. Gearhart
Robin N. Allin
W. O'Dwyer
A. R. Curreri
H. W. Wirka
K. E. Lemmer
John Z. Bowers
Robert Parkin
M. J. Musser
D. L. Williams
J. S. Supernaw
John T. Sprague
C. G. Reznichek
E. M. Burns
T. J. Nereim
L. A. Osborn
Walter Urben
Robert O'Connor
W. C. Lewis
H. H. Reese
Horace K. Tenney
William Bleckwenn
E. H. Jorris
Maxine Bennett
John Doolittle
John Beyer
F. D. Bernard
Patricia McIllece
Amy Louise Hunter
C. E. Hopkins
E. P. Roemer
D. O. Simley
Abraham Aronson
Robert M. Becker
H. C. Ashman
Helen Dickie
Milton Feig
T. V. Geppert
T. A. Leonard
William Snow Miller
Andrew J. Ward
Philip Fox
Joseph Hobbins
Francis Fischer
J. B. Bowen
Norman M. Clausen
C. P. Chapman
A. D. Anderson
R. B. Anderson
C. W. Aageson
Robert B. Ainslie
David Atwood
John Allen
H. W. Bane
Wm. H. Bartlett
P. P. Bell
Robert L. Beilman
E. A. Birge
George A. Benish
J. G. Bohorfoush
John V. Berger, Jr.
A. J. Boner
George A. Berglund

F. F. Bowman
Frank D. Bernard
P. A. Brehm
John A. Beyer
S. J. Briggs
T. W. Boldons
B. I. Brindley
Henry Brown
D. M. Britton
A. W. Bryan
John A. Buesseler
C. F. Burke
Mead Burke
Myra Burke
R. E. Burns
Edward M. Burns
Charlotte Calvert
William J. Cain
Eugenia Cameron
Homer M. Carter
R. E. Campbell
Marie L. Carns
H. M. Carter
Samuel L. Chase
J. K. Chorlog
L. R. Cole
R. F. Collins
M. J. Coluccy
R. T. Cooksey
Arch E. Cowley
H. M. Coon
O. H. Coontz
Garrett A. Cooper
Wm. P. Crowley, Jr.
John L. Coryell
Gordon Davenport
Helen P. Davis
Adrian W. Davis
R. R. Davis
F. A. Davis
Matthew D. Davis
F. K. Dean
David L. Dean
J. C. Dean
James L. Dean
James P. Dean
Hervey Dietrich
Gerald J. Derus
W. B. Dimond
Donald G. Dieter
J. E. Dollard
Charles A. Doehlert
A. Z. Domine
Peter A. Duehr
I. G. Ellis
T. C. Erickson
I. S. Evans
G. H. Ewell
Robert X. Farrell
L. Fauerbach
F. A. Fike
John H. Flinn
W. A. Focke
Oscar Foseid
C. A. Fosmark
Mark A. Foster
Ruth C. Foster
Arno H. Fromm
N. A. Frankenstein
J. W. Gale
J. T. Gallagher
W. J. Ganser
F. D. Geist
Laurence T. Giles
Farrell F. Golden
Peter B. Golden
J. E. Gonce, Jr.
E. S. Gordon
J. A. Grab
H. P. Greeley
H. L. Greene
M. F. Greiber
Frances Grimstad
E. H. Grumke
H. M. Guilford
George C. Hank
Doralea R. Harmon
Cornelius Harper
C. S. Harper

Samuel B. Harper
J. W. Harris
John R. Healy
Wm. G. Healy
F. A. Hellebrandt
R. J. Hennen
O. V. Hibma
William B. Hobbins
L. E. Holmgren
T. D. Hunt
Francis L. Hummer
J. A. Hurlbut
V. B. Hyslop
Alexander M. Iams
W. H. Jaeschke
Don R. Janicek
Frederick G. Joachim
A. C. Johnson
E. M. Juster
Fritz Kant
H. M. Kay
E. B. Keck
Jay P. Keepman
W. C. Keettel, Jr.
Thomas Kemp
W. H. Krehl
Gerald G. Kring
Palmer R. Kundert
E. C. Kurtz
C. L. Lacke
James F. Land
R. D. Lange
W. F. Lappley
Frank C. Larson
J. H. Lee
Edmund R. Liebl
W. T. Lindsay
L. V. Littig
Kenneth R. Loeffer
W. F. Lorenz
Harold N. Lubing
William V. Luetke
William H. Lyon
J. G. MacKenzie
Howard W. Mahaffey
J. P. Malec
G. J. Maloof
G. V. Marlow
W. H. Marsden
H. E. Marsh
M. G. Masten
J. C. McCarter
D. W. McCormick
S. A. McCormick
John P. McDermott
K. B. McDonough
Lester McGary
James McIntosh
R. L. McIntosh
Leonard J. McKenzie
Walter E. Meanwell
O. O. Meyer
W. E. Meisekothen
W. S. Middleton
James E. Miller
F. E. Mohs
J. N. Moore
W. A. Mowry
John J. Mueller
William C. Mussey
E. E. Neff
E. R. Nelson
M. E. Nesbit
W. M. Nesbit
Carl N. Neupert
J. R. Newman
E. J. Nordby
Dorothy W. Oakley
W. H. Oatway, Jr.
G. E. Oosterhous
O. S. Orth
B. K. Ozanne
H. K. Parks
William B. Parsons, Jr.
L. W. Paul
Joseph Pessin
M. P. Peters
Donald A. Peterson
E. A. Pohle

Donald O. Price
Lawrence R. Prouty
Margaret Prouty
K. L. Puestow
Edward F. Purcell
A. A. Quisling
G. D. Quisling
R. A. Quisling
Sverre Quisling
Leland Reeck
H. L. Reed
R. J. Reuter
C. G. Reznichek
A. J. Richtsmeier
Hania W. Ris
J. H. Robbins
Sion C. Rogers
Bryan H. Roisum
J. G. Russo
Royal Rotter
Edward K. Ryder, Jr.
John A. Salick
Etheldred L. Schafer
E. R. Schmidt
E. F. Schneiders
A. P. Schoenenberger
Claude F. Schroeder
Alwin E. Schultz
Addie M. Schwittay
E. L. Sevringhaus
H. H. Shapiro
Richard W. Shropshire
A. A. Sinaiko
Russel P. Sinaiko
I. R. Sisk
E. E. Skroch
Dean Barton Smith
Max M. Smith
Arthur M. Sonneland
Lindley V. Sprague
George G. Stebbins
W. W. Stebbins
John R. Steeper
A. C. Stehr
Lee B. Stevenson
O. A. Steinnon
Charles W. Stoops
Robert A. Straughn
Glen J. Stuesser
Henry M. Suckle
A. G. Sullivan
E. S. Sullivan
Charles R. Taborsky
John R. Talbot
W. A. Tanner
Hertha Tarrasch
F. B. Taylor
H. K. Tenney
N. G. Thomas
M. J. Thornton
A. R. Tormey, Jr.
Albert Tormey. Sr.
T. W. Tormey, Jr.
H. Trautmann
M. Trautmann
J. Kent Tweeten
J. G. Van Gemert
C. O. Vingom
S. P. Vinograd
G. H. Vogt
J. G. Waddell
Walter L. Washburn
Annette C. Washburne
Wm. L. Waskow
R. M. Waters
J. B. Wear
H. P. Weiland
E. G. Welke
May R. Wells
W. A. Werrell
R. M. Wheeler
Raymond E. Whitsitt
James M. Wilke
D. L. Williams
H. N. Winn
M. H. Wirig
Richard C. Wixson
Everet H. Wood
William H. Ylitalo

MARINETTE:

J. M. Bell
C. E. Koepp
A. T. Nadeau
K. G. Pinegar
C. H. Boren
J. W. Boren
G. R. Duer
H. L. Jorgenson
J. V. May
H. F. Schroeder
R. W. Shaw
J. D. Zeratsky

MARSHFIELD:

Robert S. Baldwin
N. J. Helland
F. A. Boeckman
L. A. Copps
K. H. Doege
P. F. Doege
S. E. Epstein
William Hipke
R. W. Mason
G. L. McCormick
E. J. McGinn
A. L. Millard
R. P. Potter
J. R. Talbot
C. A. Vedder
H. A. Vedder
J. B. Vedder
J. S. Vedder
J. M. Wickham
R. H. Wink
T. E. Wyatt

MILWAUKEE:

J. S. Ackerman
Wm. Ackermann
J. J. Adamkiewicz
H. K. B. Allebach
L. T. Allen
D. J. Ansfield
M. J. Ansfield
K. B. Appleby
J. L. Armbruster
P. E. Aszman
Alexander Augur
D. C. Ausman
H. R. Ausman
C. F. Aussendorf
T. J. Aylward
Louis Babby
E. C. Bach
J. A. Bach
M. J. Bach
R. J. Bach
E. A. Bachhuber
C. H. Bachman
E. A. Backus
C. A. Baer
V. L. Baker
B. J. Baumle
S. A. Baranowski
H. E. Bardenwerper
J. S. Barnes
J. J. Barrock
C. W. Baugh
E. L. Baum
A. J. Baumann
C. H. Baumgart
R. W. Beck
W. T. Becker
Harry Beckman
J. M. Beffel, Jr.
E. J. Behnke
E. L. Belknap
C. E. Bellehumeur
R. W. Benton
E. W. Bentzien
J. E. Bercey
R. D. Bergen
G. J. Bergmann

L. A. Bernhard
E. L. Bernhart
Alfred Beutler
E. P. Bickler
J. H. Biller
S. E. Biller
E. A. Birge
B. J. Birk
J. F. Blair
H. H. Blanchard
S. S. Blankstein
W. P. Blount
R. W. Blumenthal
J. V. Bolger
M. C. Borman
Max Bornstein
S. L. Bornstein
N. W. Bourne
L. M. Boxer
Robert Boyle
Louis Brachman
J. L. Brizard
C. F. Broderick
J. J. Brook
G. V. I. Brown
Dirk Bruins
H. R. Brukhardt
R. O. Brunkhorst
D. H. Bruns
W. A. Brussock
E. A. Brzezinski
C. L. Budny
T. H. Burbach
G. F. Burgardt
C. H. Burnett
W. W. Busby
M. B. Byrnes
Stephen Cahana
P. L. Callan
H. J. Cannon
Eben J. Carey
G. A. Carhart
E. E. Carl
E. F. Carl
W. J. Carson
J. M. Carter
I. I. Cash
W. T. Casper
G. E. Ceci
R. D. Champney
J. D. Charles
B. P. Churchill
E. A. Clasen
E. M. Cleary
David Cleveland
C. J. Coffey
S. E. Coffey
J. J. Colgan
G. E. Collentine
P. J. Collopy
J. E. Conley
J. P. Conway
E. F. Cook
H. E. Cook
C. J. Corcoran
I. I. Cowan
J. A. Cox
E. J. Craite
R. S. Cron
C. J. Crottier
H. A. Cunningham
P. M. Currer
J. G. Curtin
Eleanor Cushing
Einar Daniels
F. E. Darling
F. E. Darling, Jr.
S. J. Darling
I. Z. Davidoff
H. G. Decker
N. D. Demeter
A. V. de Neveu
F. D. Derse
J. S. Devitt
C. O. Diamond
J. O. Dieterle
C. C. Differt
M. C. Dishmaker
August Doerr

L. H. Donath
F. E. Drew
Arnold Drexel
H. N. Dricken
M. F. Drozewski
J. R. Dundon
G. O. Dunker
C. F. Dunn
C. G. Dunst
U. J. Durner
H. J. Dvorak
C. W. Eberbach
C. M. Echols
W. J. Egan
C. R. Eichenberger
P. L. Eisele
E. Eisenberg
J. J. Eisenberg
L. A. Eisenberg
P. J. Eisenberg
D. V. Elconin
E. M. End
J. A. Enright
Norbert Enzer
P. S. Epperson
Ely Epstein
F. J. Erdlitz
G. R. Ernst
C. A. Evans
E. P. Evans
S. M. Evans
E. L. Everts
B. L. Fabric
V. S. Falk
H. J. Farrell
F. J. Fechter
M. N. Federspiel
L. H. Feiman
N. N. Fein
S. M. Feld
R. H. Feldt
G. H. Fellman
M. Fernan-Nunez
J. P. Fetherston
Charles Fidler
L. M. Fisher
G. F. Fitzgerald
R. E. Fitzgerald
Wm. Fitzgibbon
H. R. Foerster
O. H. Foerster
L. J. Foley
J. W. Fons
W. B. Ford
Richard Foregger
C. A. H. Fortier
G. W. Fox
M. J. Fox
M. S. Fox
W. H. Frackelton
E. Franklin
I. Franklin
S. N. Franklin
D. D. Frawley
P. G. Fray
G. H. Friedman
R. A. Frisch
J. A. Froelich
A. H. Fromm
M. E. Gabor
R. E. Galasinski
R. W. Garens
J. G. Garland
J. L. Garvey
J. J. Gaunt
U. E. Gebhard
Sara G. Geiger
N. A. Gendlin
E. O. Gertenbach
R. T. Gilchrist
L. T. Gilmer
R. P. Gingrass
W. P. Glisch
Nathan Goldberg
J. S. Goodman
P. P. Goodman
A. H. Goodsitt
A. C. Gorder
J. S. Gordon

135

E. H. Gramling
H. J. Gramling
J. J. Gramling
J. J. Gramling, Jr.
A. W. Gray
A. I. Greenberg
R. M. Greenthal
J. C. Griffith
John Grill
J. J. Grimm
A. R. F. Grob
E. C. Grosskopf
E. E. Grossmann
L. L. Mossmann
W. F. Grotjan
W. E. Grove
V. A. Gudex
J. W. Guepe
L. H. Guerin
G. J. Gumerman
E. B. Gute
E. F. Guy
Denis Guzzetta
M. M. Guzzetta
V. J. Guzzetta
J. E. Habbe
E. A. W. Habeck
J. E. Haberland
B. T. Haessler
F. H. Haessler
C. B. Hake
R. M. Hall
J. G. Halser
A. W. Hankwitz
W. J. Hanley
H. T. Hansen
J. W. Hansen
Ervin Hansher
G. H. Hansmann
Henry Harder
Maurice Hardgrove
C. F. Hardy
L. J. Hargarten
C. W. Harper
E. T. Harrington
T. L. Harrington
J. F. Haug
H. P. Haushalter
L. E. Haushalter
H. M. Hawkins
H. J. Heeb
H. W. Hefke
F. C. Heidner
E. C. Heifetz
J. V. Heil
E. A. Heipp
H. A. Heise
T. A. Heller
Edwin Henes, Jr.
J. A. Heraty
A. H. Hermann
W. L. Herner
A. J. Hertel
J. V. Herzog
S. G. Higgins
Howard High
W. A. Hilger
R. I. Hiller
S. J. Hiller
G. A. Hipke
L. W. Hipke
M. M. Hipke
J. S. Hirschboeck
H. B. Hitz
John B. Hitz
B. A. Hoermann
F. J. Hofmeister
A. A. Holbrook
A. T. Holbrook
S. W. Hollenbeck
A. J. Hood
J. J. Horwitz
W. J. Houghton
T. J. Howard
G. E. Howe
H. H. Huber
W. W. Hume
J. R. Hurley
John Huston

E. P. Huth
J. F. Imp
Robert Irwin
Edward Jackson
E. B. Jacobson
R. A. Jefferson
J. M. Jekel
E. J. Jelenchick
J. A. Jenner
Louis Jermain
W. M. Jermain
M. A. Jochimsen
A. W. Johnson
C. G. Johnson
Frances Johnson
H. W. Johnson
J. H. Johnson
T. L. Johnston
W. A. Joseph
T. A. Judge
C. D. Jurss
Joseph Kahn
A. J. Kampmeier
A. M. Kane
J. K. Karr
K. E. Kassowitz
A. L. Kastner
L. W. Kaufman
E. M. Kay
W. M. Kearns
G. F. Kelly
W. R. Kennedy
E. J. Kettelhut
E. J. Kiefer
A. D. Kilian
G. S. Kilkenny
J. J. King
J. M. King
J. L. Kinsey
C. A. Kissinger
A. C. Kissling
J. T. Klein
J. W. Kleinboehl
W. J. Kleis
M. G. Klumb
A. H. Knudson
M. J. Koch
J. P. Koehler
S. E. Kohn
Arthur Kovacs
F. J. Kozina
F. H. Kramoris
L. H. Kretchmar
Morris Kretchmar
F. A. Kretlow
H. T. Kristjanson
F. J. Kritter
G. A. Kriz
Rose Kriz-Hettwer
E. R. Krumbiegel
J. L. Kruszewski
A. A. Krygier
W. L. Krygier
S. L. Krzysko
H. J. Kuhn
M. J. Kuhn
A. S. Kult
C. M. Kurtz
A. F. Kustermann
O. E. Lademan
A. W. Ladewig
H. C. Ladewig
A. H. Lahmann
F. J. Lambeck
D. H. Lando, Jr.
V. F. Lang
A. R. Langjahr
W. A. Langmack
W. L. LeCron
P. A. Lee
G. W. Leitch
Abram Levine
Marian Lewis
Ben Lieberman
W. C. Liefert
George Light
O. R. Lillie
M. C. F. Lindert
E. T. Lobedan

C. W. Long
Oscar Lotz
D. M. Loughlin
I. B. Love
J. B. Ludden
B. A. Lungmus
M. J. Lustok
A. J. Macht
F. E. MacInnis
W. L. MacKedon
J. A. MacKenzie
F. W. Mackoy
M. F. MacRae
F. W. Madison
J. D. Madison
O. W. Maercklein
B. J. Mainekoff
J. Y. Malone
R. W. Mann
F. C. Margoles
Milton Margoles
L. S. Markson
S. M. Markson
C. R. Marlewski
C. R. Marquardt
W. H. Marshall
E. W. Martens
H. G. Martin
E. W. Mason
N. E. McBeath
John McCabe
J. O. McCabe
Edith McCann
M. T. McCormack
F. X. McCormick
T. F. McCormick
C. F. McDonald
R. E. McDonald
W. J. McKillip
N. W. McKittrick
F. B. McMahon
H. O. McMahon
J. F. McNary
W. D. NcNary
Salvatore Megna
D. D. Mehigan
Abraham Melamed
F. J. Mellencamp
G. E. Meloy
H. Mendeloff
E. H. Mensing
A. N. E. Merten
P. J. Merten
C. Messmer
E. W. Miller
H. L. Miller
H. B. Miner
S. R. Mitchell
F. C. Mock
S. Moglowsky
S. M. Mollinger
J. M. Molsberry
L. J. Monaghan
A. Montgomery
R. P. Montgomery
J. E. Morgan
S. F. Morgan
R. E. Morter
S. A. Morton
Elizabeth Moxley
A. J. Muckerheide
F. R. Muehlhaus
R. J. Muenzner
J. E. Mulsow
F. H. Munkwitz
F. D. Murphy
J. A. Murphy
W. J. Murphy
A. L. Natenshon
Harold Nebel
G. W. Neilson
J. D. Nelson
W. V. Nelson
Mary Neville
C. L. Newberry
C. J. Newcomb
C. H. Nichols
P. J. Niland
T. M. Northey

A. C. Nugent
H. G. Oakland
P. E. Oberbreckling
T. W. O'Donovan
J. J. O'Hara
E. B. O'Leary
A. H. Olsen
Maurice Olsen
H. J. Olson
T. S. O'Malley
W. P. O'Malley
E. J. O'Neill
Frederick Oswald
Owen Otto
D. W. Ovitt
G. C. Owen
J. D. Owen
J. B. Ozonoff
F. J. Pallasch
E. J. Panetti
H. E. Panetti
C. F. Park
A. J. Patek
T. M. Paulbeck
A. W. Peelen
J. W. Pegram
T. J. Pendergast
P. H. Perlson
M. G. Peterman
B. J. Peters
L. M. Peters
L. T. Peyton
E. N. Pfeffer
R. G. Piaskoski
J. J. Pink
Samuel Plahner
A. A. Pleyte
H. W. Pohle
W. S. Polacheck
Saul Pollack
Albert Popp
H. W. Powers
A. A. Presti
H. H. Prudowsky
G. J. Pugh
P. J. Purtell
R. F. Purtell
A. J. Quick
E. W. Quick
Allen Rabin
W. F. Ragan
Forrester Raine
T. G. Randolph
R. T. Rank
J. W. Rastetter
A. J. Raymond
I. B. Reifenrath
C. C. Reinke
E. H. Rettig
Frank Rettig
M. J. Reuter
A. F. Rheineck
E. L. Rice
E. M. Rice
G. J. Rich
F. W. Riehl
C. S. Rife
D. F. Rikkers
H. F. Ringo
D. W. Roberts
H. P. Robinson
H. S. Roby
J. N. Rock
R. W. Roethke
A. F. Rogers
E. H. Rogers
M. F. Rogers
T. H. Rolfs
M. K. Rosenbaum
A. I. Rosenberger
S. Rosenthal
F. A. Ross
J. P. Rowan
A. J. Ruppenthal
L. F. Ruschhaupt
R. J. M. Russell
P. W. Ryan
W. A. Ryan
H. B. Sadoff

T. P. Saketos
S. S. Salinko
O. A. Sander
A. J. Sanfelippo
I. J. Sarfatty
J. C. Sargent
L. C. Sass
G. F. Savage
G. T. Savage
W. J. Schacht
R. E. Schade
A. A. Schaefer
E. J. Schelble
J. P. Schelble
K. Schlaepfer
B. H. Schlomovitz
E. H. Schlomovitz
B. Schlossmann
F. E. Schlueter
U. A. Schlueter
A. C. Schmidt
E. C. Schmidt
H. G. Schmidt
J. A. Schmidt
Felix Schmit
Louis Schmit
G. Schmitt
A. C. Schnapp
L. Schneeberger
C. C. Schneider
C. R. Schneider
C. S. Schneider
R. C. Schodron
C. M. Schoen
B. Schoenkerman
E. A. Scholter
G. M. Scholz
O. P. Schoofs
R. P. Schowalter
A. J. Schramel
H. T. Schroeder
J. C. Schroeder
F. J. Schubert
F. X. Schuler
Irwin Schulz
H. S. Schumacher
H. C. Schumm
A. G. Schutte
E. D. Schwade
A. B. Schwartz
S. F. Schwartz
L. R. Schweiger
G. J. Schweitzer
W. A. Schweitzer
S. J. Seeger
F. W. Seegers
A. G. Seelman
J. J. Seelman
Elizabeth Seiler
F. S. Selle
Nicholas Senn
Ulrich Senn
Joseph Shaiken
G. O. Shaner
A. M. Shapiro
M. W. Sherwood
J. F. Shimpa
Michael Shutkin
H. W. Shutter
H. P. Siekert
S. J. Silbar
A. W. Sivyer
Nathan Slutzky
J. W. Smith
L. D. Smith
R. H. Smuckler
S. B. Spilberg
M. M. Spitz
Robert Sponner
A. D. Spooner
R. P. Sproule
T. L. Squier
L. P. Stamm
W. S. Stanley
R. M. Stark
J. D. Steele, Jr.
J. S. Stefanez
C. M. Steiner
E. K. Steinkopff

Louis Stern
W. L. Stetner
R. E. Stockinger
F. A. Stratton
G. D. Strauss
W. H. Studley
G. A. Sullivan
J. M. Sullivan
J. H. Sure
E. H. Sutter
A. A. Sverdlin
W. M. Sweemer
S. J. Sweet
J. E. Szymarek
H. Tabachnick
G. K. Tallmadge
E. H. Tashkin
E. L. Taube
J. G. Taylor
G. F. Tegtmeyer
R. A. Teschan
A. F. Tessier
E. L. Tharinger
G. E. Thill
E. X. Thompson
R. D. Thompson
A. H. Thorstensen
J. A. Thranow
E. M. Tillson
O. E. Toenhart
T. L. Tolan
N. O. Tomkiewicz
S. S. Torcivia
F. G. Treskow
J. C. Troxel
J. W. Truitt
Millard Tufts
V. C. Turner
C. F. Turney
M. H. Uhley
A. A. Unger
B. E. Urdan
J. M. Usow
L. B. Uszler
W. Van de Erve
L. J. Van Hecke
L. A. Vander Linde
Henry Veit
L. H. Verch
A. J. Verdone
Chester Wade
P. C. Wagner
R. C. Waisman
I. J. Waldman
L. J. Walker
Adolf Wallner
G. Wallschlager
W. B. Walton
R. C. Warner
B. Warschauer
R. G. Washburn
T. D. Watry
A. J. Weber
G. H. Wegmann
N. J. Wegmann
W. F. Weingart
L. R. Weinshel
F. G. Weisfeld
L. A. Weisfeldt
S. C. Weisfeldt
R. R. Weller
W. P. Wendt
D. E. Wenstrand
D. J. Werner
J. J. Werner
R. C. Westhofen
S. H. Wetzler
G. E. Whalen
L. M. Wieder
M. E. Wiese
R. P. Wiesen
J. P. Wild
J. B. Wilets
J. C. Wilets
E. D. Wilkinson
Donald Willson
C. A. Wilske
W. J. Winnemann
W. G. Winter

Carlton Wirthwein
D. H. Witte
W. C. F. Witte
S. H. Wolter
H. H. Wright
J. F. Wyman
Aaron Yaffe
A. E. Yanke
A. F. Young
J. J. Zaun, Jr.
S. E. Zawodny
Helen J. Zillmer
C. Zimmermann
S. S. Zintek
J. F. Zivnuska
W. P. Zmyslony
D. J. Zubatsky
J. C. Zuercher
H. O. Zurheide

NEENAH:

M. N. Pitz
S. R. Beatty
C. G. Kirchgeorg
G. R. Anderson
H. L. Baxter
H. F. Beglinger
Gail Broberg
F. O. Brunckhorst
J. P. Canavan
O. F. Foseid
R. C. Lowe
R. A. Moon
I. E. Ozanne
G. W. Peterson
R. H. Quade
T. D. Smith
G. H. Williamson

MENASHA:

W. B. Hildebrand
G. B. Hildebrand
P. T. O'Brien
G. E. Forkin
F. G. Jensen
R. A. Jensen
G. N. Pratt, Jr.
L. S. Shemanski

MONROE:

W. J. Fencil
L. G. Kindschi
C. E. Baumle
N. E. Bear
W. G. Bear
J. H. Bristow
L. E. Creasy
H. E. Fillbach
W. B. Gnagi
W. B. Gnagi, Jr.
F. W. Kundert
L. A. Moore
D. D. Ruehlman
J. A. Schindler
R. J. Zach

OCONOMOWOC:

W. D. James
D. C. Wilkinson
J. D. Wilkinson
J. F. Wilkinson
M. R. Wilkinson
Phillip Wilkinson
Albert Rogers
Owen C. Clark
J. S. Giffin
James C. Hassall
A. J. Loughnan
G. R. Love
D. A. Morrison
T. H. Nammacher

I. T. Stemper
P. B. Theobald

OSHKOSH:

M. H. Steen
S. J. Graiewski
S. R. Beatty
R. H. Bitter
Burton Clark
W. E. Clark
F. G. Connell
E. F. Cummings
Q. H. Danforth
M. J. Donkle
R. O. Ebert
J. M. Fraser
M. C. Haines
H. J. Haubrick
L. O. Holmes
J. M. Hogan
D. G. Hugo
H. W. Kleinschmit
A. G. Koehler
J. J. Kronzer
R. V. Kuhn
H. J. Lee
W. N. Linn
J. W. Lockhart
G. V. Lynch
C. A. Meilicke
J. V. Meli
A. A. Mendez
H. H. Meusel
G. C. Owen
E. B. Pfefferkorn
H. A. Romberg
J. E. Schein
L. M. Smith
G. A. Steele
J. F. Stein
R. F. Wagner
W. A. Wagner
W. P. Wheeler
E. B. Williams
P. E. Wright

PRAIRIE DU CHIEN:

William Beaumont
E. M. Dessloch
Milton Trautmann
W. S. Cusik
H. L. Shapiro
C. A. Armstrong
T. F. Farrell
J. J. Kane
H. H. Kleinpell
E. H. Lechtenberg
G. M. Sargeant
O. E. Satter

RACINE:

R. O. Peterson
W. C. Hanson
R. J. Schacht
L. E. Fazen
Louis E. Fazen, Jr.
F. M. Hilpert
A. W. Adamski
J. M. Albino
H. B. Beeson
H. N. Boyer
H. G. Brehm
H. J. Brehm
C. F. Browne
W. E. Buckley
F. C. Christensen
C. E. Constantine
K. W. Covell
J. C. Docter
Louis J. Fazen, Jr.
S. J. Faber
G. N. Gillett
J. A. Gosman

C. K. Hahn
P. R. Hahn
W. C. Hanson
T. C. Hemmingsen
J. F. Henken
H. C. Hilker
J. H. Hogan
H. W. Howe
R. D. Jamieson
Beatrice O. Jones
K. C. Kehl
H. B. Keland
C. L. Kline
Wm. F. Konnak
R. W. Kreul
R. M. Kurten
L. M. Lifschutz
A. M. Lindner
F. B. Marek
H. C. Miller
A. L. Nelson
R. O. Peterson
T. J. Pfeffer
E. C. Pfeifer
A. S. Pfeiffer
O. W. Pfeiffer
F. W. Pope
Gorton Ritchie
G. L. Ross
W. C. Roth
G. L. Rothenmaier
E. W. Schacht
G. O. Schaefer
Grace Schenkenberg
E. J. Schneller
L. N. Schnetz
R. C. Thackery
I. F. Thompson
I. N. Tucker
E. von Buddenbrock
B. L. von Jarchow
N. B. Wagner
G. W. Walter
F. A. Wier
R. S. Wright

RHINELANDER:

W. S. Bump
W. K. Simmons
Marvin Wright
T. M. Haug
Frances A. Cline
W. F. Gager
A. F. Harter
L. F. Kaiser
V. Komasinski
C. A. Richards
I. E. Schiek
I. E. Schiek, Jr.
H. J. Westgate

SHEBOYGAN:

T. J. Gunther
F. A. Nause
F. A. Nause, Jr.
P. B. Mason
Keith Keane
L. M. Simonson
B. F. Eckardt
R. M. Senty
A. B. C. Bock
J. J. Boersma
J. F. Carey
F. Eigenberger
O. A. Fiedler
W. A. Ford
A. E. Genter
B. J. Glaubitz
Carl Greenstein
Ludwig Gruenwald
H. H. Heiden
G. J. Hildebrand
W. G. Huibregtse
G. J. Juckem
J. A. Junck

A. J. Knauf
G. E. Knauf
F. K. Kolb
J. F. Kovacic
Siegfried Kraft
J. W. McRoberts
William G. Meier
V. F. Neu
W. H. Neumann
L. F. Pauly
G. H. Scheer
A. J. Schmitt
E. G. Schott
W. M. Sonnenburg
C. A. Squire
G. H. Stannard
C. T. Tasche
J. A. Tasche
L. W. Tasche
Wesley Van Zanten
William Van Zanten
C. J. Weber
R. L. Zaegel

STEVENS POINT:

M. G. Rice
R. W. Rice
George Anderson
H. A. Anderson
W. A. Gramowski
H. P. Benn
W. F. Cowan
E. P. Crosby
A. G. Dunn
W. W. Gregory
F. C. Iber
E. E. Kidder
F. R. Krembs
J. A. Litzow
F. A. Marrs
S. R. Miller
W. C. Sheehan
P. N. Sowka
R. J. Stollenwerk
C. von Neupert
Erich Wisiol

SUPERIOR:

V. E. Ekblad
C. J. Picard
J. W. Easton
C. W. Giesen
Milton Finn
H. A. Sincock
John G. Heisel
F. G. Johnson, Jr.
E. G. Stack
M. S. Averbrook
L. W. Beebe
E. E. Carpenter
C. H. Christiansen
R. E. Christiansen
H. B. Christiansen
T. J. Doyle
C. T. Droege
Conrad Giesen
J. R. Goodfellow
Wm. Edwin Ground
B. J. Hathaway
F. G. Johnson, Jr.
J. C. Kyllo
J. W. McGill
J. M. Meyers
E. A. Myers
T. J. O'Leary
H. J. Orchard
S. H. Perrin
F. C. Sarazin
W. H. Schnell
D. R. Searle

M. H. Wall
J. H. Weisberg
A. G. Wilcox

WATERTOWN:

F. C. Haney
T. C. Abelmann
W. C. Becker
E. W. Bowen
H. P. Bowen
E. E. Burzynski
O. F. Dierker
A. C. Hahn
F. E. Kosanke
H. G. Mallow
E. A. Miller
A. C. Nickels
L. H. Nowack
L. W. Nowack
W. S. Waite
R. P. Welbourne
F. H. Zimmerman

WAUKESHA:

A. J. Williams
P. E. Campbell
W. B. Campbell
B. M. Caples
J. Christianson
Gwilym Davies
R. E. Davies
C. C. Edmondson
J. C. Frick
H. A. Gantz
A. J. Hodgson
D. H. Lando
E. L. Lochen
J. B. Noble
W. H. Oatway
F. M. Scheele
H. F. Sydow
U. J. Tibbitts
S. M. Welsh
M. J. Werra
A. J. Williams
C. A. Wood
F. J. Woodhead
F. G. Zietlow

WAUSAU:

R. B. Larsen
C. M. Yoran
A. H. Stahmer
E. B. Brick
A. W. Boslough
A. W. Burek
H. H. Christensen
V. E. Eastman
H. H. Fechtner
H. R. Fehland
R. F. Fisher
J. V. Flannery
E. E. Flemming
J. M. Freeman
W. C. Frenzel
F. H. Frey
D. M. Green
M. L. Jones
R. H. Juers
E. P. Ludwig
E. M. Macaulay
H. F. Martini
F. C. Prehn
P. Z. Reist
J. F. Smith
S. M. B. Smith
G. H. Stevens
J. K. Trumbo
O. M. Wilson

WAUWATOSA:

K. J. Winters
A. R. Altenhofen
A. L. Banyai
H. B. Benjamin
A. V. Gadden
V. J. Cordes
J. S. Cutler
E. L. Dallwig
E. R. Daniels
N. F. Dettmann
L. J. Deysach
D. D. Feid
R. M. Fellows
L. L. Fifrick
J. J. Furlong
J. F. Gates
W. H. Gebert
R. T. Hansen
R. A. Hershberg
M. Q. Howard
F. R. Janney
G. H. Jurgens
Michael Kasak
F. H. Kehlnhofer
E. C. Kocovsky
W. T. Kradwell
B. K. Lovell
C. W. Osgood
E. F. Peterson
L. W. Ramlow
James Regan
H. M. Roberts
B. A. Ruskin
H. W. Sargeant
H. T. Schroeder
L. A. Seymer
E. J. Shabart
Samuel Wick
L. H. Ziegler

WEST ALLIS:

S. B. Black
E. V. Brumbaugh
T. T. Couch
R. H. Frederick
K. Friedbacher
J. W. Fulton
F. C. Heinan
W. C. Hermann
L. H. Hirsh
G. H. Hoffmann
W. P. Klopfer
M. C. Malensek
F. N. Nimz
R. A. Nimz
I. J. Sarfatty
R. H. Smits
M. P. Stamm
Armin Steckler
C. S. Stern
W. L. Stranberg
R. A. Toepfer
L. A. Van Ells
J. J. Wilkinson
Thomas Willett

WISCONSIN RAPIDS:

R. E. Garrison
E. C. Glenn
E. G. Barnet
L. J. Bennett
Edward Hougen
J. J. Looze
Wallace Nelson
F. J. Pomainville
F. X. Pomainville
L. C. Pomainville
J. J. Smullen
Donald Waters

G. G. Shields, Abbotsford; A. J. Bosse, Ableman; R. C. Faulds, Abrams; A. J. Harris and Harry Shapiro, Adams; I. M. Bemis and F. J. Naylen, Adell; F. J. Bongiorno and L. L. Weismiller, Albany; B. J. Bertram and W. W. Witcpalek, Algoma; R. S. Fisher, Allenton; M. O. Bachhuber,

Alma; Thomas Arneson, Almena; W. B. Cornwall, K. K. Ford, F. L. Whitelark, V. C. Kremser, and I. L. Waterman, Amery; J. F. Dorsch, Amherst; Elizabeth Comstock, B. C. Dockendorff, J. P. Skroch, and F. T. Weber, Arcadia; R. E. Hunter, W. B. Williams, Argyle; G. J. Bachhuber, H. M. Bachhuber, and Lewis Frick, Athens; O. G. Moland, and H. F. Prill, Augusta; Bertha Reynolds, Avoca; C. A. Olson, B. Kunny, and G. B. Swenson, Baldwin; K. P. Ruppenthal and M. W. Ward, Bangor; H. M. Templeton, C. C. Post, K. A. Ruethin, H. H. Schlomovitz, and R. C. Smith, Barron; J. K. Shumate, H. G. Mertens, Henry Hannum, Bayfield; L. F. Morneau, Bear Creek;

W. F. Donlin, Belleville; J. C. Hubenthal, Belmont; P. W. Leitzell, Benton; H. C. Koch, John Koch, L. J. Seward, G. C. Stone, Mildred M. Stone, and A. J. Wiesender, Berlin; R. E. Boldt, Big Bend; H. H. Ainsworth, Birchwood; E .E. McCandless, Birnamwood; L. J. Laird, Black Creek; Irwin Krohn, Robert Krohn, and K. F. Manz, Black River Falls; Carl Milchen, Blair; C. T. Clauson, D. F. Hudek, and J. J. Sazama, Bloomer; H. J. McLaughlin, Bloomington; H. V. Bancroft, Blue Mounds; M. W. Randall, Blue River; H. M. Klopf and J. H. Terlinden, Bonduel; C. S. Hayman, M. J. Ruzicka, E. H. Spiegelberg, and F. S. Tuffley, Boscobel; H. M. Hull, Brandon; J. R. Goelz, F. B. Vande Loo, and A. J. Wagner, Brillion; E. J. Mitchell and M. W. Stuessy, Brodhead; R. G. Raymond and M. F. Ries, Brownsville;

M. L. Whalen, Bruce; M. W. Alcorn, J. F. Bennett, H. W. Granzeau, L. O. Mastalir, R. A. Mullen, W. J. Murawsky, and F. F. Newell, Burlington; C. E. Zenner, B. J. Haines, Cadott; E. O. Ronneburger, Cambria; K. K. Amundson and G. E. Bilstad, Cambridge; C. F. Cronk, Cameron; H. C. Johnson, Camp McCoy; O. F. Guenther and L. A. Hoffmann, Campbellsport; E. J. Kerscher, Casco; C. H. Cremer and N. M. Mauel, Cashton; A. C. Rempe, Cassville; J. M. Kelley, Cato; P. B. Blanchard, O. J. Hurth, O. W. Hurth, and H. M. Katz, Cedarburg; L. A. Van Altena and A. Voskull, Cedar Grove; G. B. Noyes, Centuria; W. H. Remer and J. R. Richter, Chaseburg; R. W. Adams, Chetek; E. W. Humke, Kenneth Humke, J. W. Goggins, N. J. Knauf, and J. J. Minahan, Chilton;

L. A. Campbell, Jr., Clayton; A. N. Nelson and L. A. Campbell, Clear Lake; E. N. Reinert, Cleveland; W. O. Thomas, Clinton; Irving Auld, R. F. Braun, H. S. Caskey, W. H. Finney, E. A. Miller, J. H. Murphy, and C. A. Topp, Clintonville; C. R. Brillman, Cobb; E. A. Meill, Cochrane; A. L. Schemmer and H. H. Christofferson, Colby; L. H. Graner, Coleman; C. A. Cooper and O. M. Felland, Colfax; H. M. Caldwell, C. F. Cheli, A. J. Frederick, J. A. Murdoch, and E. M. Poser, olumbus; A. A. Solberg, Coon Valley; J. H. Foster, Cornell; D. V. Moffet, G. W. Ison and H. C. Marsh, Crandon; W. E. L. Froggatt; Cross Plains; F. M. Bair and H. E. Fillbach, Cuba City; E. J. Ackerman, J. M. Fine, S. H. Kash, C. V. Kierzkowski, B. Krueger, M. Landsberg, E. M. Lawler, C. D. Partridge, and H. S. Smith, Cudahy; S. O. Lund and R. C. Thompson, Cumberland; H. M. Levin, Darien; E. D. McConnell, L. L. Olson, N. A. McGreane, R. B. Quinn, and H. O. Shockley, Darlington; C. L. Ingwell, Deerfield; T. W. Dasier, Deer Park; E. P. Carlton, De Forest; H. T. Barnes and L. C. J. Olsen, Delafield; G. A. Smiley, C. V. Bachelle, N. F. Crowe, J. W. Doughty, T. L. Jacobson, H. J. Kenney, F. L. O'Keefe, H. J. Werbel, and C. A. Wright, Delavan;

F. J. Hager, C. T. Michna, H. J. Schilling, A. P. Schoenenberger, W. H. Vosburgh, Denmark; N. M. Kersten, J. P. Lenfestey, and R. M. Waldkirch, De Pere; H. A. Bolstad and L. M. Gorenstein, De Soto; H. M. Buckner, W. P. Hamilton, H. H. Morton, William Reese, and H. M. Walker, Dodgeville; F. P. Foley, Dorchester; W. R. Notbohm, Dousman; R. J. Bryant, and R. R. Richards, Durand; J. J. Fitzgerald, Eagle; C. O. Lindstrom, O. R. McMurry, and R. A. A. Oldfield, Eagle River; S. G. Meany and T. J. O'Leary, East Troy; J. H. Hardgrove, Eden; H. A. Schulz, Edgar; G. F. Burpee, A. T. Shearer, F. E. Shearer, and W. C. Sumner, Edgerton; P. J. Dailey, Elcho; F. A. Jackson, Eldorado; J. E. Martineau, Elkhart Lake; M. G. Helmbrecht, J. A. Rawlins, E. T. Ridgway, E. D. Sorenson, and J. H. Young, Elkhorn; A. Aanes, C. R. Cannon, and V. W. Nordholm, Ellsworth; R. Y. Wheelihan, Elm Grove; A. L. Breed, Elmwood; C. A. Vogel, Elroy; C. O. Rogne, Ettrick; R. J. Gray, J. P. Guilfoyle, and S. S. Sorkin; F. F. Zboralske, Fall Creek; F. O. Hunt, Fall River; M. A. Bailey, E. C. Howell, T. H. Marsden, and W. H. Schuler, Fennimore; R. J. Dalton, Fifield;

J. R. Harvey, Footville; P. J. Wollersheim, Forest Junction; J. G. Hirschboeck, Forestville; H. O. Caswell, F. A. Gruesen, L. H. Gueldner, O. H. Hanson, James Russell, J. J. Harris, R. C. Morris, J. R. Venning, and Will Young, Fort Atkinson; F. C. Skemp, Fountain City; E. S. Elliott, Fox Lake; G. A. Dockery, Franksville; R. G. Arveson, W. C. Andrews, W. A. Fischer, R. M. Moore, D. A. Maas, and K. F. Johnson, Frederic; C. P. Arnoldussen, Fremont; G. F. Treadwell, Friendship; R. L. Alvarez, H. A. Jegi, E. P. Rohde, and F. T. Younker, Galesville; E. T. Ackerman and S. R. Boyce, Gays Mills; Griffith Jones, Genesee Depot; L. H. Baldwin and W. R. Berg, Gillett; A. P. Hable and A. L. Cramp, Gilman; John Hansen, Glenbeulah; R. C. Love and C. F. McCusker, Glenwood City; F. J. Ansfield, Glidden; C. H. Kinsbury, Goodman; K. F. Pelant, C. A. Balkwill, and C. H. Kalb, Grafton; R. R. Rath and R. H. Slater, Granton;

G. E. Baldwin and J. A. Kelly, Green Lake; E. A. Titel, Greenleaf; W. A. Olson and M. V. Overman, Greenwood; F. L. Litzen, Gresham; N. M. Wilson, Grimms; D. F. Pierce and R. C. Wolf, Hales Corners; C. A. Olson, Hammond; J. G. Hoffmann, F. W. Lehmann, T. F. Loughlin, M. E. Monroe, and F. W. Sachse, Hartford; R. T. Hansen, G. W. Brewer, F. L. Grover, and E. A. Reddeman, Hartland; J. C. Baker, Hawkins; V. A. Lookanoff, Hawthorne; D. H. Callaghan, E. H. Dufour, and G .E. Wesche, Hayward; C. B. Strauch, Hazel Green; D. F. Doyle and M. T. Erickson, Highland; P. H. Hansberry, R. S. MacKechnie, and J. J. Rouse, Hillsboro; E. A. Petzke, Hixton; S. B. Marshall, Hollandale; L. E. Hanson, Holmen; C. S. Bloom, G. G. Drescher, and J. H. Karsten, Horicon; W. A. Adrians, and W. H. Towne, Hortonville; J. W. Livingstone, G. E. Bourget, and J. E. Newton, Hudson; T. J. Hambley, D. J. Martinetti, and Will Egan, Hurley; P. A. Panetti, Hustisford; C. F. Peterson, D. R. Peterson, and B. R. Walske, Independence; W. F. Wilker, Iola; E. C. Quackenbush, Iron Ridge; H. E. Froede, Jackson; J. C. Brewer, A. A. Busse, C. J. Garding, R. W. Quandt, C. E. Quandt, and A. H. Robinson, Jefferson; F. A. Wendt, Johnson Creek; G. W. Reis, Junction City; H. J. Heath and C. L. Qualls, Juneau; A. E. and A. M. Bachhuber, C. D. and G. L. Boyd, G. J. Flanagan, and John Hogan, Kaukauna;

R. R. Rivard, Keshena; R. G. Edwards and N. E. Hausmann, Kewaskum; D. B. Dana, L. E. Dockry, E. W. Witcpalek, F. J. and W. M. Wochos, Kewaunee; F. P. Knauf, D. F. Nauth, and S. P. O'Donnell, Kiel; C. G. Maes, Kimberly; R. C. Montgomery, King; M. D. Cottingham and C. C. Gascoigne, Kohler; W. B. A. Bauer, L. M. Lundmark, W. F. O'Connor, H. F. Pagel, and Woodruff Smith, Ladysmith; F. F. Gallin and O. Sporleder, La Farge; C. J. Brady, E. D. Hudson, Dean Jeffers, and W. H. MacDonald, Lake Geneva; G. E. Eck, Phillip Leicht, M. G. Peterson, and E. A. Schoenecker, Lake Mills; H. W. Carey, J. H. Fowler, J. D. Glynn, R. C. Godfrey, E. M. Houghton, and Elgie Kraut, Lancaster; G. E. Carroll and E. G. Ovitz, Laona;

D. W. Curtin, J. H. Doyle, and W. C. Verbick, Little Chute; R. J. Groves and G. H. Irwin, Lodi; E. L. Jewell, Loganville; A. P. Hable, Loyal; S. C. Peterson, Luck; R. K. Irvine and W. J. Irvine, Manawa; C. E. Kampine, Marathon; J. H. May, Maribel; F. M. Mulvaney and R. E. Van

140

Schaick, Marion; D. P. Cupery and E. S. Sinaiko, Markesan; O. F. Partridge, Mattoon; J. H. Vedner, J. S. Hess, Mauston; M. E. Royce, F. G. Bachhuber, and G. A. Parish, Mayville; I. Schultz, Mazomanie; E. B. Elvis, D. M. Norton, L. E. and R. C. Nystrum, Medford; C. W. Lockhart, Mellen; I. H. Lavine, Melrose; M. K. Green, August Sauthoff, and W. J. Urben, Mendota; E. W. Burkhardt, W. G. Domann, Menomonee Falls, G. E. Hoyt, and A. J. Schloemer, Menomonee Falls; C. H. Buckley, F. E. Butler, I. V. Grannis, J. A. Halgren, D. T. Long, Wm. Lumsden, A. E. McMahon, P. A. Quilling, B. J. and R. J. Steves, Menomonie; A. Kremers and Wm. G. Hiatt, Mercer; W. F. Austria, L. J. and W. H. Bayer, H. G. Hinckley, F. H. Kelley, F. C. Lane, K. A. Morris, J. N. Millenbak, Bjarne Ravn, and E. O. Ravn, Merrill; M. F. Stricker and O. S. Orth, Middleton; L. B. Bergstrom, J. F. Maser, and E. T. Rechlitz, Milltown; G. E. Crosley and Milton D. Davis, Milton; T. L. Vogel, Milton Junction; C. L. White, H. D. Ludden, Mineral Point; G. W. Huber, J. P. Sprague, and T. G. Torpy, Minocqua; R. C. Darby and C. J. Skwor, Mishicot; J. J. Gillette, L. B. Hansen, B. F. Johnson, and D. S. Sharp, Mondovi;

R. F. Inman and L. W. McNamara, Montello; M. P. Ohlsen, Monticello; M. W. Garry and J. M. Pierpont, Montreal; E. F. Butler and J. A. Jackson, Mosinee; J. M. Baasen and J. F. Miller, Mount Calvary; M. T. Morrison, Judson Forman and A. S. Thompson, Mount Horeb; W. J. Voellings, Mukwonago; W. E. Klochow and J. D. Walsh, Muscoda; G. J. Kelm, Muskego; H. A. and J. H. Frank, M. V. Overman, H. W. Housley, M. C. and Sarah D. Rosecrans, T. N. Thompson, Neillsville; O. A. Backus, C. J. and H. G. Pomainville, Nekoosa; R. C. Richardson, Neopit; H. F. Weber, Newburg; J. A. Looze, New Franklins; S. J. A. Francois, E. V. Hicks, and E. D. McQuillin, New Glarus; F. J. Brown, F. P. Larme, A. C. Engel, and H. C. Krohn, New Holstein; Brand Starnes, New Lisbon; M. A. Borchardt, G. P. Dernbach, J. W. Monsted, F. J. Pfeifer, and H. C. Schmallenberg, New London; J. H. Armstrong, E. M. Drury, and O. H. Epley, New Richmond; Edward McCormack, Niagara;

T. J. Buckley, North Freedom; F. J. Donnelly, North Lake; J. S. Allen, Norwalk; H. A. Aageson, R. J. Rogers, C. R. Kwapy, H. W. Pankow, A. F. Slaney, F. E. Zantow, and A. N. Tousignant, Oconto; L. E. Rauchschwalbe, R. J. Goggins, G. W. Krahn, and H. F. Ohswaldt, Oconto Falls; L. J. Schoenbechler and V. G. Springer, Omro; G. D. Reay, Onalaska; G. C. Devine, Ontario; E. T. Hougen, Oostburg; E. S. Johnson and T. H. Joyner, Oregon; G. W. Belting and E. R. McNair, Orfordville; L. J. Weller, H. J. Jeronimus, Jr., and L. O. Simenstad, Osceola; O. Knutson and R. N. Leasum, Osseo; Harold Brosswell, B. H. Dike, Owen; R. S. Ingersoll, Oxford; E. E. Bertolaet, Palmyra; J. Chandler and H. E. Gillette, Pardeville; J. D. Leahy, J. L. Murphy, and E. A. Riley, Park Falls; A. E. Belitz and G. E. Bryant, Pepin; J. M. Bell and H. W. Haasi, Peshtigo; L. W. Egloff, K. P. Hoel, and J. P. Kelly, Pewaukee; J. J. Lutz, Phelps; W. P. Sperry, H. B. Norviel, J. L. Rens, and D. S. Van Hecke, Phillips; Hart Beyer and E. C. Glenn, Pittsville; P. H. Fowler, Plain; B. P. Ingersoll, Plainfield; C. H. Andrew, Wilson Cunningham, J. L. Moffett, H. L. Doeringsfeld, C. M. Schuldt, J. W. Conklin, F. A. Soles, and C. H. E. Wheeler, Platteville; O. H. Anderson, Plum City; A. J. Brickbauer, H. F. Deicher, L. C. Dietesch, J. F. Mueller, L. Gruenwald, A. C. Radloff, A. W. Sieker, and C. M. Yoran, Plymouth;

A. J. Batty, E. A. Doersch, J. P. Doersch, J. P. Harkins, C. W. Henney, J. W. MacGregor, W. A. Taylor, and E. F. Tierney, Portage; Arnold Barr, J. F. Walsh, W. H. Drissen, C. P. Kauth, R. K. Pomeroy, G. S. Cassels, and C. C. Stein, Port Washington; Wm. J. Kelly, Potosi; R. B. Pelkey, Pound; R. B. Dryer and W. J. Focke, Poynette; G. C. Stimpson, Poy Sippi; Milton Trautmann, K. D. L. Hannan, and E. M. Randall, Prairie du Sac; G. E. MacKinnon, Prentice; G. M. Dill and H. J. Laney, Prescott; G. G. Mueller, Princeton; L. E. Gallette, J. R. Goggins, and V. J. Shippy, Pulaski; E. H. Federman, A. W. Jones, and E. W. Vetter, Randolph; T. E. Malloy and J. A. Russell, Random Lake; R. C. Darby, Red Granite; J. J. Rouse, O. V. Pawlisch, R. G. Knight, E. V. Stadel, and E. D. Stanton, Reedsburg; E. C. Cary, Reedsville; W. E. Bargholtz, Reeseville; A. S. Horn, Rib Lake; D. L. Dawson, J. F. Maser, E. J. Hatleberg, O. E. and W. B. Rydell, Rice Lake; T. J. Kern, Richfield; G. B. and G. H. Benson, W. R. Coumbe, Dayton Hinke, L. C. Davis, C. F. Dull, W. C. Edwards, R. E. Housner, George Parke, Jr., L. M. Pippin, B. I. Pippin, D. J. Taft, and C. A. Sholtes, Richland Center; W. C. Maas and W. A. Pease, Rio;

D. F. Cole, C. P. Hazeltine, O. A. Dittmer, J. M. Johnson, R. H. Jones, S. J. Leibenson, Orvil O'Neal, C. U. Senn, and E. L. Watson, Ripon; P. H. Gutzler, R. U. Cairns, Chalmer Davee, C. A. Dawson, and C. E. J. McJilton, River Falls; A. M. Ford, Roberts; M. M. Scheid, Rosendale; V. A. Benn, Rosholt; H. J. Kief, St. Cloud; H. C. Caldwell, C. A. Kelly, and J. A. Riegel, St. Croix Falls; H. A. Bachhuber and T. W. Walsh, Sauk City; E. J. Konop, Sawyer; G. R. Hammes, Seneca; R. C. Groendahl, V. J. Hittner, and L. H. Sieb, Seymour; H. C. Marsh, Frederick Bauer, A. A. and R. C. Cantwell, L. W. Peterson, W. J. Schutz, A. J. Sebesta, D. A. Jeffries, and C. E. Stubenvoil, Shawano; H. J. Hansen and A. G. Pfeiler, Sheboygan Falls; E. R. Hering and D. V. Moen, Shell Lake; G. M. LaCroix, Shiocton; S. A. J. Ennis and T. J. Nereim, Shullsburg; C. A. DeWitt, Silver Lake; L. F. Sherman, Siren; K. F. Prefontaine, Slinger; W. A. Sannes, Soldiers Grove; S. L. Chojnacki, R. R. Crigler, G. P. Dempsey, G. S. Flaherty, H. H. Oberfeld, C. L. Rumph, and W. A. Sickels, South Milwaukee; M. T. Morrison, South Wayne; D. C. and S. D. Beebe, Harry Mannis, C. S. Phalen, S. M. Roberts, J. M. Scantleton, H. H. Williams, and H. H. Williams, Jr., Sparta;

H. T. Callahan, Spencer; G. N. Lemmer and A. E. Muccilli, Spooner; Frank Nee and C. M. Wahl, Spring Green; H. P. and J. M. Conway, Spring Valley; R. E. Graber and A. W. Overgard, Stanley; H. E. Perrin, Star Prairie; R. H. Schmidt, Statesan; J. A. Knauf, Stockbridge; H. A. Keenan, A. L. Olson, R. F. Schoenbeck, and A. T. Smedal, Stoughton; L. R. Pfieffer, E. F. Winter, Strum; J. G. Beck, D. E. Dorchester, H. D. Grota, F. C. Huff, and J. O. Muehlhauser, Sturgeon Bay; F. G. Peehn, Sturtevant; J. M. McCabe, E. J. Nelson, and L. W. Peterson, Sun Prairie; J. S. Dougherty, Spring; E. C. Van Valin, Sussex; P. F. Lagenfeld, Theresa; A. H. C. Carthaus, J. W. Rock, and H. F. Scholz, Thiensville; F. P. Neis, Thorp; F. E. Hypes, Three Lakes; A. J. Gates, Tigerton; A. R. Bell, V. H. Cremer, L. G. Scheurich, J. S. Mubarak, E. A. Schmidt, T. J. Sheehy, C. E. Kozarek, and A. E. Winter, Tomah; G. R. and R. G. Baker, and W. C. McCormick, Tomahawk; R. T. Shima, Turtle Lake; A. W. Kozelka, R. E. Martin, L. J. Moriarty, G. A. Rau, and A. P. Zlatnik, Two Rivers; C. C. Atherton, R. W. McCracken, E. Reinardy, and Gordon J. Schulz, Union Grove; E. W. Huth and R. S. Simensen, Valders; H. A. Andersen, Verona; C. A. Morrow and George Parke, Viola; H. and L. F. Gulbrandsen, R. S. Hirsch, A. E. Kuehn, H. R. Ludden, S. J. Martin, R. A. Starr, C. H. and W. M. Trowbridge, Viroqua;

O. S. Tenley, Wabeno; W. W. Coon and T. J. Kroyer, Walworth; John Jehl and H. C. Wesche, Washburn; R. J. Dietz, F. A. Malone, and David Wigod, Waterford; S. C. Allen and J. F. Dennis, Waterloo; J. M. Grinde, W. R. Marquis, and O. E. Toenhart, Waunakee; M. O. Boudry, A. M. Christofferson, L. G. Patterson, Owen Larson, and Sam Salan, Waupaca; F. T. Clark, A. J. Hebenstreit, J. F. Klepfer, A. R. Remley, C. P. Reslock, R. E. Schrank, and K. A. Swartz, Waupun;

U. M. Horswell and J. M .Rose, Wausaukee; A. A. Beck and G. L. Karnopp, Wautoma; L. E. Rauchschwalbe, Wauzeka; Wm. H. Cochrane, Wayside; David Maas, Webster; K. T. Bauer, E. L. Bernhardt, S. J. Driessel, R. O. Frankow, A. H. Heidner, P. M. Kauth, and H. M. Lynch, West Bend; C. M. Strand, P. T. Bland, Westby; C. S. Bolles and R. B. Lenz, West De Pere; H. Y. Frederick, J. G. Moss, Westfield;

R. H. Goedecke and G. F. Wakefield, West Salem; L. F. Corry and E. A. Weller, Weyauwega; R. L. MacCornack, N. S. Simons, and J. C. Tyvand, Whitehall; D. R. Notbohm, White Lake; D. A. Gutheil, Whitelaw; Walter Mauthe and R. H. Miller, Whitewater; S. L. Hadden, Wild Rose; R. F. Sanders and C. Y. Wiswell, Williams Bay; C. H. Feasler, B. J. Hughes, R. C. Morrison, J. T. Petersik, and L. B. Perssion, Winnebago; T. E. Kilkenny, Winneconne; J. H. Houghton and C. J. Radl, Wisconsin Dells; H. E. Breckenridge and E. F. Hafemeister, Wisconsin Veterans Home; J. W. Johnson, Withee; M. C. Crane and E. E. Evenson, Wittenberg; Wm. G. Hiatt, Kate Pelham Newcomb, Woodruff; C. W. Hughes, C. W. Rhea, and F. B. Landis, Wood; Julius Blom, Woodville.

∫

RET'D FEB 20 1986

JAN 17 1995